AA CLED
WI CLOUDS
SHE CAM

60 Lyrics frae the Chinese

About the Author

Brian Holton, born in Galashiels in 1949, and educated at the Universities of Edinburgh and Durham, has published more than twenty books and pamphlets of translated poetry, including Yang Lian's *Venice Elegy* (Edizioni Damocle, 2019) and *Narrative Poem* (Bloodaxe Books, 2017). In 2021, he was awarded the inaugural Sarah McGuire Prize for Poetry Translation for Yang Lian's *Anniversary Snow* (Shearsman Books, 2019). Holton's collection of classical poems in Scots, *Staunin Ma Lane*, was published by Shearsman Books in 2016, and his *Hard Roads an Cauld Hairst Winds: Li Bai an Du Fu in Scots* by Taproot Press in early 2022. *Hard Roads an Cauld Hairst Winds* was nominated for Scots Book of the Year, Scots Language Awards 2022.

He has won other prizes both for his own poetry in Scots and for his translations into both Scots and English. He is a recovering academic who taught Chinese language and literature at Edinburgh, Durham and Newcastle, and translation at Newcastle and the Hong Kong Polytechnic University. He has given lectures, readings and workshops at universities and major literary festivals in the UK, Spain, Italy, Holland, New Zealand, China, the USA, and Canada. He lives in Melrose in the Scottish Borders, close to where he was born.

AA CLED
WI CLOUDS
SHE CAM

60 Lyrics frae the Chinese

BRIAN HOLTON

With a Foreword by Kathleen Jamie

THE IRISH PAGES PRESS
2022

Aa Cled Wi Clouds She Cam
is first published in hardback
on 30 October 2022.

The Irish Pages Press
129 Ormeau Road
Belfast BT7 1SH
Ireland

www.irishpages.org

Editors: Chris Agee and Kathleen Jamie

Typeset in 13/16.5 pt Monotype Perpetua and Adobe Kaiti.
Designed and composed by RV, Belfast. Printed by Bell & Bain, Glasgow.

A CIP catalogue record for this book
is available from The British Library.

Dust-jacket photograph:
Robert Sutherland.

ISBN: 978-1-8382018-7-6

Also by Brian Holton

AS TRANSLATOR

Non-Person Singular: Collected Shorter Poems (1994)

Water on the Border (1994)

China Daily (1995)

Where the Sea Stands Still: New Poems (1999)

Notes of a Blissful Ghost: Selected Poems (2002)

Concentric Circles (2005)

Pisces Rising (2008)

Lee Valley Poems (2009)

*Jade Ladder: A Bloodaxe Anthology of
Contemporary Chinese Poetry* (2012)

Paper Cuts (2015)

A Massively Single Number (2015)

Staunin Ma Lane: Chinese Verse in Scots and English (2016)

Narrative Poem (2017)

Anniversary Snow (2019)

Venice Elegy (2019)

*Hard Roads an Cauld Hairst Winds:
Li Bai an Du Fu in Scots* (2022)

A Tower Built Downwards (Bloodaxe Books, 2023)

Acknowledgements

I would very much like to thank Chris Agee and Kathleen Jamie for their enthusiastic support and the adoption of this book, and also the editors of *Lallans* and *Causey*.

A big shout to Bill Herbert, Joan Hewitt, Mark Husmann, Andy Gardner, and the rest of the Tyneside Pig Board Zoomers, to Sandip Mehta in Montreal, Pino Baffi in Rome, Monika Holton in Fife, Andrea Streit in Paris, Elizabeth Morrell and Cosima Bruno in London, who all helped keep me functioning during lockdown.

As I was working on these translations, Bach's unaccompanied cello suites, Purcell's *In Nomines* and *Fantasias* for Viols, and Robert Carver's masses and motets provided my soundtrack.

CONTENTS

FOREWORD
Kathleen Jamie

To a non-Chinese speaker like myself, one who can barely understand what is meant by "oblique" or "level" tones, one who boggles at ideograms, it's astonishing to encounter Brian Holton's simple statement "I took the book off the shelf and began to read".

The book he so casually opened is the *300 Song Ci* – a text written in Classical Chinese, which, he tells me, is as different from Modern Standard Chinese, or Mandarin, as Latin is from Italian. The *Ci* are songs or lyrics over 1,000 years old, but still familiar to Chinese school students, the way the contents of Palgrave's *Golden Treasury* once were to ours.

Such was Brian Holton's reading: ancient Chinese song lyrics. Imagine being able to read, and say, this: 宋詞三百首.

The *Ci* (say *tsuh*), are poems which were originally written to extraordinary formal demands. There are an astonishing 800 preordained shapes that a poet might choose from, for his (usually his) lyric to inhabit. We might compare it to our own varieties of sonnet, of which we have several, but not 800. The

Ci have set patterns of line length, and sound-patterns created by arrangements of the aforementioned tones. There must be rhyme. The poems are furthermore intended to be sung to pre-existing tunes. Hence the stipulation in this book of the "air" any given lyric should be sung to, though these tunes themselves are mostly lost. Only their delightful names remain.

All of this matters, and none of it does. Though it may cause Maister Holton some chagrin, we can set aside that linguistic and poetic complexity and go directly to his poems in Scots. He has translated 60 of the 300 *Ci* available. We can enjoy them as beautiful, yearning poems new-born in our language. (English is given as a fall-back, until the ear becomes accustomed to the Scots, if needs be.)

What he gives us is not the demotic Scots we know from many contemporary novels. Rather he composes in literary, poetic, Scots. The poems sound modern because, despite the formality of the originals, his translations read as free verse. They are without set metre or rhyme-schemes. The poetry resides in the sounds, the beguiling diction, the half-hidden alliterations and consonances and slant rhymes, the varying long and short lines and "mirroring" of stanzas (note these latter two features exist in the originals).

Though a thousand years and several thousand miles separate the original works from these new translations, we can recognise the landscapes and the emotions. A lone, often lonely, sometimes wry voice sings forth in a way which is easy on the ear and touching to the heart. The poems are filled with exile and flowers, loneliness and gardens, boats and rivers, drink, mountains and clouds. We know the pangs of regret. We recognise the images:

A vast o watter,
Geese on the links,
That glifft, birl an skail.

There is an interiority to the language which shows us – for it seems we're aye needing to be shown – what Scots can do. How it can reach into subtle emotional registers, into intimacies, into soft musicalities.

Why are these poems so totally at home in Scots, like doves which have flown here from afar and settled into a local doo-cot? Is there something about the ancient Chinese lyrics themselves that allow for this, or is it Brian's skill at naturalising them? The answer must be "both". Although it's quite different, I'm reminded of the way the New Testament sounds so right and alive in Lorimer's Scots translation. Like Lorimer's, Brian Holton's Scots is unforced, unselfconscious, deft and – dare we say – thoroughly enjoyable?

How wonderful it would be to hear these poems sung in Scots, to airs new or old.

Brian Holton's abilities were of course developed through years of scholarship, practice and graft. But like those of a musical virtuoso, they appear innate, a wholly natural flourishing. A Scots speaker since childhood, Brian read Chinese Studies at university. He has spent his career with the language, translating and teaching in the UK and in China and Hong Kong, before "retiring" to his native Borders. To my mind, the books he has produced in recent years, of Chinese works owersett into Scots, are a major achievement and gift to his native land.

Here is *"Aa Cled Wi Clouds She Cam"*. Sae clivver, sae awfae bonnie.

Thou lytill quair, be ewir obedient,
Humble, subject and simple of entent
Before the face of ewiry connyng wicht.
I knaw quhat thou of rhetorike hes spent.

William Dunbar *The Golden Targe*

Note On Pronunciation

Chinese names are transliterated using the standard *Hanyu Pinyin* system.

Vowels have roughly Italian values, except for the following:

> /u/ after /j/, /q/, /x/, /y/ – German /ü/
> /i/ after /zh/, /ch/, /sh/, /r/, /z/, /c/, /s/ – slightly higher than Scots *grund*, or NZ *fish*.

Most initial consonants will be intelligible with Scots values, except for the following:

> /c/ – Scots /ts/
> /q/ – Scots /ch/ as in *chin*
> /r/ – like English /r/ with curled-up tongue, not flapped as in Scots
> /x/ – a light /sh/ with the tongue behind the bottom teeth.

THE SANGS

錢惟演
QIAN WEIYAN (962-1034)[1]

Remembered now as a *bon vivant*, a convivial patron of poets, and a bibliophile with an enormous library, Qian was of royal birth, son of the last king of the Yangtse Delta state of Wu-Yue, who surrendered to the Song Dynasty in 978. He had a long career in the mandarinate, on both the military and civil sides.

---

1 Some sources give his birth as 977, then have him entering into his first civil service post the following year, which seems unlikely, to say the least. Wang Zhong places his birth in the 3rd year of the Xianping reign period, i.e. 962CE (*Songci Sanbai Shou*, 1989, p1).

木蘭花

城上風光鶯語亂。
城下煙波春拍岸。
綠楊芳草幾時休？
淚眼愁腸先已斷。

情懷漸覺成衰晚。
鸞鏡朱顏驚暗換。
昔年多病厭芳尊，
今日芳尊惟恐淺。

Ti the air o *MAGNOLIA FLOURISH*

On the citie waa-heid a scene o yatterin yalla-yites,
At the citie waa-fuit the skite o drowy waves on the
    springtime strand;
Green sauchs an sweet gress, hou lang will they lest?
Begrutten een an sorrae i the wame, hairt langsyne broken.

In her sel she's lairnin hou she's dwynit throu the years,
Wi a gliff she sees her rosy cheek chyngit aa unkent in the
    keekin-gless.
Years bypast, aye no-weill, she scunnert at the drink,
Nou aa she's feart o is her bonnie bicker tuimin.

To the air of *MAGNOLIA BLOSSOM*

On top of the city wall a scene of chattering orioles,
At the foot of the city wall the slap of misty waves
    on the spring shore;
Green willow and sweet grass, how long will they last?
Tear-stained eyes and sorrow in the belly,
    heartbroken long ago.

In herself she's learning how she's declined over the years,
With a start she sees her rosy cheek in the mirror
    has changed unnoticed.
Years ago, always ill, she sickened of drinking,
Now all she fears is her pretty goblet emptying.

———————

范仲淹
FAN ZHONGYAN (989-1052)

Essayist, poet, and reforming Confucian politician, he grew up in poverty, studying for the Civil Service examinations in a Buddhist temple. His ground-breaking poetry, versatile and deeply-felt, laid the groundworks of the new Northern school. His most lasting social achievement was to endow a foundation in 1050 to fund the education of clan members, which endured until 1760.

蘇幕遮

碧雲天，
黃葉地，
秋色連波，
波上寒煙翠。
山映斜陽天接水，
芳草無情，
更在斜陽外。

黯鄉魂，
追旅思，
夜夜除非，
好夢留人睡。
明月樓高休獨倚，
酒入愁腸，
化作相思淚。

Ti the air o *SMUDGIE-BUNNET*[2]

Clouds in the blue lift,
Yalla leafs on the yirth;
Hairst-time colours jink an swee on the swaws,
On the swaws a cauld blae rouk;
Hills shinin in dayset whaur watter meets the lift,
Hairtless the sweet gress,
Faur ayont the dayset.

Dowie hame-seik sowl,
Huntit wi oorie fremmitness,
Nicht eftir nicht forbye
The yae bonnie dream at convoys a bodie ti sleep.
Dinna lean yir lane in a high touer ablow a bricht mune,
When drink's intil a hairtsair wame,
It chynges ti luve-seik tears.

---

2 蘇幕遮 *Sumuzhe* is a loan word from a Silk Road language, such as Tokharian or Sogdian. It was the title of a song, and may have been the name of a Central Asian singer or dancing-girl, or may also have referred to a specific kind of head gear, ornament, or hat. I render it phonetically.

To the air of *SMUDGIE-BONNET*

Clouds in the blue sky,
Yellow leaves on the earth;
Harvest-time colours dance on the waves,
On the waves a cold grey mist;
Hills shine in sunset where water meets the sky,
Heartless the sweet grass,
Far beyond the sunset.

Doleful home-sick soul,
Haunted with uneasy foreignness,
And night after night, too,
That one lovely dream that will conduct someone to sleep.
Don't you lean alone in a high tower under a bright moon,
When drink gets into a sore heart,
It changes to lovesick tears.

———————————

漁家傲

塞下秋來風景異，
衡陽雁去無留意。
四面邊聲連角起，
千嶂里，
長煙落日孤城閉。

濁酒一杯家萬里，
燕然未勒歸無計。
羌管悠悠霜滿地，
人不寐，
將軍白髮征夫淚。

Ti the air o *FISHER'S PRIDE*

Hairst-time comes eerie-lookin ti the Mairches,
Wild geese at Tronbricht win awa wi nae mind to stey;
Aawhaur the souns o the borderlan, horns even-on blawin;
Amang a thousan craigs,
In the lang haar o dayset the Lane Peel's steikit ticht.

Yin bicker o drumlie yill ten thousan mile frae yir ain hous,
Wi the Khangai Hills onyowden yit there'll be nae ettlin
        for hame;
Cranreuch haps the land as Droverfowk's pipes
        soun dreich an lang;[3]
Yin bodie isna sleepin:
Our white pow'd general's greetin a sodger's tears.

---

3 The ethnonym 羌 Qiāng denoted a Central Asian people whose name meant something like "shepherd", if their name is Tibeto-Burman, or, if Indo-European, "charioteer".

To the air of *FISHERMAN'S PRIDE*

Autumn comes strangely to the Marches,
Wild geese at Tronbright go with no intent to stay;
Everywhere the sounds of the borderland,
  horns always blowing;
Among a thousand crags,
In the long mists of sunset the Lone Peel Tower's
  shut up tight.

One beaker of cloudy ale ten thousand miles
  from your own house,
With the Khangai Hills still unyielded there's no plan
  for going home;
Hoarfrost wraps the land as Droverfolk pipes
  sound dreary and long;
One person isn't sleeping:
Our white-haired general weeps a soldier's tears.

御街行

紛紛墮葉飄香砌，
夜寂靜，
寒聲碎。
真珠簾卷玉樓空，
天淡銀河垂地。
年年今夜，
月華如練，
長是人千里。

愁腸已斷無由醉，
酒未到，
先成淚。
殘燈明滅枕頭欹，
諳盡孤眠滋味。
都來此事，
眉間心上，
無計相迴避。

Ti the air o *WALKIN KINGSGATE*

A pirlin rowth o faa'n leafs wreaths the palace steps,
Lythe an lown's the nicht,
Wi juist the orra souns o cauld winter;
Pearl hingers rowit up an the Jowelt Laft tuim,[4]
Pale's the lift, the White Strip hingin doun ti the yirth;
Ilka year this verra same nicht comes,
Mune skyrie bricht as whitest silk,
An somebodie still a thousan mile awa.

Ma sair hairt's broken an it's nae guid gettin fou,
E'en afore the drink comes
It's turnt ti tears;
The failin cruisie's smoorit, the bowsters is aa agley,
Fine weill A ken the pree o sleepin ma lane;
It comes back ay an aft ti this,
On ma brou or in ma hairt,
Nae wey A'll e'er jouk it.

---

4 i.e. an elegant apartment, a singing-girl's rooms, or a brothel.

To the air of *WALKING KING STREET*

A swirling plenty of fallen leaves wreathes the palace steps,
Silent and still's the night,
With only the odd sounds of cold winter;
Pearl curtains rolled up and the Jewel Loft empty,
Pale's the sky, the Milky Way hanging down to Earth;
Each year this very same night comes,
Moon shining bright as whitest silk,
And somebody still a thousand miles away.

My sore heart's broken and it's no good getting tipsy,
Even before the drink comes
It's turned into tears;
The failing lamp's put out, the bolsters all awry,
How well I know the taste of sleeping alone;
It all comes back to this,
On my brow or in my heart,
No way I'll ever dodge it.

———————

張先
ZHANG XIAN (990-1078)

He passed the *Jinshi* (Metropolitan Graduate) exam at the age of 41, and served in Sichuan and Gansu. Much of his innovative, elegant, refined, and sophisticated poetry is lost, as is almost all of his prose, though he was praised by and associated with some of the greatest literary figures of the age, and highly regarded for his mastery of blended expressive and imagistic elements in his *ci*.

千秋歲

數聲鶗鴃，
又報芳菲歇。
惜春更選殘紅折，
雨輕風色暴，
梅子青時節。
永豐柳，
無人盡日花飛雪。

莫把么弦撥，
怨極弦能說。
天不老，
情難絕，
心似雙絲網，
中有千千結。
夜過也，
東窗未白孤燈滅。

Ti the air o *A THOUSAN HAIRST-TIMES*

Gowks croodle-croodle,
Tellin the flouers it's time ance mair ti gie owre;
Vext for the spring, A choice a beuch o cuisten reid
    an brak it aff,
In the smaa rain the wind's gowstie,
It's the saison o green ploums;
The sauchs o Evergrowthie Gairdens,[5]
No the yae bodie there aa day, an flouers fleein
    like flauchts o snaa.

Touchna a single thairm-string,
Thae thairms can tell ma sairest o plaints;
Heaven growsna auld,
Hairt-likin's ill ti sned awa,
Hairts twynit like twa ettercap wabs,
Insnorlt wi thousans an thousans o fankles;
The nicht's gane,
The ae white lamp in the eastren winnock's smoorit.

---

5 In Luoyang, in modern Henan Province, the Western Capital of the Northern
Song Dynasty (960-1127), not the political or administrative capital, but an impor-
tant cultural centre.

To the air of A THOUSAND AUTUMNS

Cuckoos coo and coo,
Telling the flowers it's time again to rest;
Vexed for the spring, I chose a bough of faded red
    and break it off,
In the small rain the wind's blustery,
It's the season of green plums;
The willows of Evergrowing Gardens,
Not a single person there all day, and flowers flying
    like flakes of snow.

Don't touch a single string,
These strings can tell my sorest complaints;
Heaven doesn't grow old,
Love's hard to break off,
Hearts entwined like two spiderwebs,
Tangled with thousands and thousands of knots;
The night's gone,
The single white lamp in the eastern window has gone out.

———————

菩薩蠻

哀箏一弄《湘江曲》,
聲聲寫盡湘波綠。
纖指十三弦,
細將幽恨傳。

當筵秋水慢,
玉柱斜飛雁。
彈到斷腸時,
春山眉黛低。

Ti the air o *FREMMIT BODHISATTVAS*[6]

Yin pouk at the waefu zither an it's the *Hotterburn Port,*[7]
Note eftir note scrieves out the emerant waves
    o the Hotterburn;
Smaa fingers on thirteen thairms
Perjink tell owre a tale o waefu sorrae;

Her een at the foy, sweirt as the Lammas spate,
Zither-trees o jade, a skein o wild geese;
She'll play ti ma hairt braks,
Her pentit brous like twa bleck hills ablow spring rain.

---

6 Apparently named after a delegation of women from the country of Nüman
女蠻國 *(Female Foreigner Country)* which visited the Tang court, dressed, it seemed
to the Chinese, like bodhisattvas, with bouffant hair and pearl-strung blouses.
7 The 箏 *zheng* is a horizontal half-tube plucked zither with movable bridges, like
its Japanese descendant the Koto. Here port means, as it does in the Gaelic, a tune.

To the air of *FOREIGN BODHISATTVAS*

One stroke on the mournful zither and it's the *Hotterburn Air*
Note after note engraves the emerald waves
    of the Hotterburn;
Small fingers on thirteen strings
Neatly tell a tale of woeful sorrow;

Her eyes at the party, lazy as the autumn spate,
Zither-bridges of jade, a skein of wild geese;
She'll play until my heart breaks,
Her painted brows like two black hills below spring rain.

醉垂鞭

雙蝶繡羅裙，
東池宴初相見。
朱粉不深勻，
閑花淡淡春。

細看諸處好，
人人道柳腰身。
昨日亂山昏，
來時衣上雲。

Ti the air o *FOU FAAS THE WHUP*

Skirt flouert wi twa butterflees,
The foy at the eastren pule,
When first A saw her;
Rouge an pouther no owre thick onlaid,
A wild flouer pale an fine in the spring;

A gat a guid look, an she's braw in ilka wey;
Aabodie said,
Her middle's as jimp as a sauch.
Yestreen in bruckle hill gloamin
Aa cled wi clouds she cam.

To the air of *DRUNKEN FALLS THE WHUP*

Skirt embroidered with two butterflies,
The party at the eastern pool,
When first I saw her;
Rouge and powder not too thickly laid on,
A wild flower pale and fine in the spring;

I got a good look, and she's lovely in every way;
They all said,
Her waist's willow-slim.
Last night in unsettled mountain twilight
She came, all clad in clouds.

————————

一叢花

傷高懷遠幾時窮？
無物似情濃。
離愁正引千絲亂，
更東陌、
飛絮濛濛。
嘶騎漸遙，
征塵不斷，
何處認郎蹤？

雙鴛池沼水溶溶，
南北小橈通。
梯橫畫閣黃昏後，
又還是、
斜月簾櫳。
沉恨細思，
不如桃杏，
猶解嫁東風。

Ti the air o *A BUSS O FLOUERS*

Lamentin in the laft, thinkin on a bodie ferawa, when'll it end?
Naethin sae sair as the stouns o love;
The doul o twynin's like a thousan raivelt threids,
The eastrenmaist path,
The drow o flichterie sauch tossels;
Nicherin pownies' slaw wa-gaun,
An enless is the stour o the king's host:
Whaur can A speir out ma guidman's fuitsteid?

Braid an caum's Marradeuk Lochan's watters,
Wi wee cobles gaun back an forrit;
Eftir the lether ti ma pentit pavilion's heftit up
    an the gloamin's by,
Ance mair it's back ti this:
The sklentit mune on the winnock hingers,
An me whummlt wi rue, thinkin lang –
Better A wis peach or abrico flourish,
Free ti wad the eastren wind.

To the air of *A BUSH OF FLOWERS*

Lamenting in the loft, thinking of somebody far away,
    when will it end?
Nothing hurts like the pains of love;
The ache of parting is like a thousand muddled threads,
The easternmost road,
The haze of fluttering willow catkins;
With neighing ponies' slow departure,
Endless is the dust of the Imperial host:
Where can I track down my husband's footsteps?

Broad and calm are Marrowduck Pond's waters,
With little rowing boats going back and forward;
After the ladder to my painted pavilion's lifted
    and the twilight's gone,
Once again it's back to this:
The slanted moon on the window blinds,
Overcome with regrets and longings –
Better I were peach or apricot blossom,
Free to wed the east wind.

天仙子

《水調》數聲持酒聽，
午醉醒來愁未醒。
送春春去幾時回？
臨晚鏡，
傷流景，
往事後期空記省。

沙上並禽池上暝，
雲破月來花弄影。
重重簾幕密遮燈，
風不定，
人初靜，
明日落紅應滿徑。

Ti the air o *HEIVINLIE TRANSCENDAND*

Monie's the time A've heard *The Watter's Port*
    wi a dram in ma haun,
A'm sowthert o ma meridian dram, but no ma sorra,
A've convoyed the Springtime awa, but whan'll it come back?
Forenent the keekin-gless at e'en,
Doul an wae for the bygane years,
Ploys langsyne an whit cam eftir, tuim's the mindin o't.

Marrowit birds on the sauns an gloamin owre the lochan,
Clouds spleit an out comes the mune, sae flouers can daff
    wi their shaddaes;
Layer on layer o winnock-hingers,
    an the cruisie-lamp happit ticht,
Eemis is the wind,
Folk newlins wheesht,
Under the bricht mune faa'n reid leafs
    sud be clatchin the paths.

To the air of *HEAVENLY TRANSCENDENT*

Many's the time I've heard *The Water Air* with a drink
    in my hand,
I've recovered from my noon dram, but not from my sorrow,
I've seen the Springtime off, but when will it come back?
Before the looking-glass at eventide,
Wounded from the bygone years,
Long-ago fun and what followed, vain to remember it.

Paired birds on the sands and twilight on the lake,
Clouds split and out comes the moon, so flowers can flirt
with their shadows;
Layer on layer of curtains, and the oil-lamp tightly covered,
Inconstant is the wind,
Folk fall silent now,
Under the bright moon fallen red leaves
    should be filling the paths.

———————

青門引

乍暖還輕冷，
風雨晚來方定。
庭軒寂寞近清明，
殘花中酒，
又是去年病。

樓頭畫角風吹醒，
入夜重門靜。
那堪更被明月，
隔牆送過鞦韆影。

Ti the air o *THE BLAE PORT OWRECOME*

It wis warm for a wee then it turnt a thing cauld,
The blatter o rain at cam at e'en hes juist devault;
Palins in the Palace Close are lown an lanesome
    this near the Day o the Deid[8],
Gettin blin fou amang the dwynin flouers:
Here's fernyear's ailins back ance mair.

On the port-heid the pentit horns blaw waukrife in the wind,
Doublt yetts stane-dumb at the derknin:
Hou can A thole the bricht mune
Sendin the shedda o the shoo-shuggie owre the dyke again?

---

8 That is, Qingming Festival: 清明 means *clear & bright*. Also known as Tomb-Sweeping Day, this is the Chinese Day of the Dead, when tombs are visited, swept, and cleaned, and offerings made to ancestors. It takes place in early April, 15 days (half a lunation) after the Spring Equinox, as it has done for well over two thousand years.

To the air of *THE BLUE GATE REFRAIN*

It was warm for a while then it turned a little cold,
The blast of rain that came at evening has just stopped;
Railings in the Palace Courtyard are still and lonely
    so close to the Day of the Dead,
Getting drunk among fading flowers:
Here's last year's sickness back again.

On the tower the painted horns blow sleepless in the wind,
Doubled gates dumb in the twilight:
How can I endure the bright moon
Sending the shadow of the seesaw across the wall again?

———————

生查子

含羞整翠鬟，
得意頻相顧。
雁柱十三絃，
一一春鶯語。

嬌雲容易飛，
夢斷知何處。
深院鎖黃昏，
陣陣芭蕉雨。

Ti the air o *CALLER HAWS*[9]

Blatelike she fettles a cockernonie aa sperkie wi jowels,
Fair joco, aye an aft she keeks owre at uis;
Thirteen thairms on wild-guse zithertrees
Yin an bi yin wheeple the lintie's sang.[10]

Sic a denty cloud'll easy flee awa,
Whae kens whaur she'll be whan ma dreams devaul;
The gloamin's sneckit up i the howe o the close,
Wi the dreep-dreep o rain on banana leafs.

---

9 This poem is also attributed to Ouyang Xiu (1007-1072).
10 The bird is naturalised. *Cettia cantans* is a kind of Asian warbler.

To the air of *FRESH HAWTHORN BERRIES*

Shyly she straightens a cap all sparkling with jewels,
Pleased with herself, she's always peeping at me;
Thirteen strings on wild-goose zither bridges
One by one whistle the warbler's song.

Such a delicate cloud will easily fly away,
Who knows where she'll be when my dreams give over;
The twilight's locked up in the hollow of the courtyard,
With the drip-drip of rain on banana leaves.

晏殊
YAN SHU (991-1055)

A prodigy from a poor family who earned his *Jinshi* degree at 14, he was very successful as an official, rising to the prime ministerial rank of Grand Councillor, only to be dismissed at the age of 44, for unknown reasons. His home was famous as a gathering place of poets, literati, and singing-girls. His style is colloquial, thoughtful, refined and delicate, balancing melancholy and philosophical reflection.

浣溪沙

一曲新詞酒一杯，
去年天氣舊池臺，
夕陽西下幾時回？

無可奈何花落去，
似曾相識燕歸來，
小園香徑獨徘徊。

Ti the air o *WESHIN BURNIE SAUNS*

A new sang an a bicker o wine,
Fernyear's weather again, an the Stank Deas like afore,
The sun dwynes westawa at dayset, but when'll it retour?

Flouers faa, an deil the thing ti be dune:
Yince, A kent the swallas wad win hame again,
Back an forrit A gaun on ma wee gairden path
        atween the flouers.

To the air of *WASHING STREAMLET SANDS*

A new song and a beaker of wine,
Last year's weather again, and the Pond Podium
    just like before,
The sun sinks in the west at nightfall,
    and when will it return?

Flowers fall, and nothing to be done:
Once, I knew the swallows would come home again,
Back and forth I go on my little garden path
    between the flowers.

———————

浣溪沙

一向年光有限身，
等閒離別易消魂，
酒筵歌席莫辭頻。

滿目山河空念遠，
落花風雨更傷春，
不如憐取眼前人。

Ti the air o *WESHIN BURNIE SAUNS*

The braw years wir endit instanter:
Ornar twynins an pairtins'll easy whummle a bodie,
Dinna nay-say owre aften at the ceilidh or the coggie-cowpin.

Missin yin at's ferawa's vain whan hills an watters fill yir ee,
Faain flouers in the blatterin rain'll gar ye rue
      spring's end the mair,
Better ti lou the bodie ye see afore ye.

To the air of *WASHING STREAMLET SANDS*

The good years ended all at once:
Ordinary separations and partings will easily overwhelm you,
Don't say no too often at ceilidh or roistering.

Missing someone who's far away is vain when hills and waters
    fill your eyes,
Falling flowers in the battering rain will make you regret
    spring's end still more,
Better to love the one you see before you.

清平樂

紅箋小字，
說盡平生意，
鴻雁在雲魚在水，
惆悵此情難寄。

斜陽獨倚西樓，
遙山恰對簾鉤。
人面不知何處，
綠波依舊東流。

Ti the air o *LOWN PLEISURS*[11]

Wee words on reid letter paper,
Tell out hou A lou'd ye aa ma days;
The're swan-geese in the clouds, fish in the watter[12] –
But A'm great-hairtit wi ill-ti-scrieve feelins.

In the settin sun A hing ma lane in the westren touer,
Forenent the hingers, the ferawa hills;
A kenna whaur ma jo's face has gane,
But the green swaws rowe eastawa, same as aye.

---

11 This translation was Highly Commended, Scots Language Society *Sangschaw* competition, 2021.
12 Both are kennings for messengers who might carry letters and news.

To the air of *QUIET PLEASURES*

Little words on red letter paper,
Tell out how I loved you all my days;
There are swan-geese in the clouds, fish in the waters –
But I'm heavy-hearted with feelings impossible to write.

In the setting sun I lean alone in the western tower,
Beyond the curtain, the faraway hills;
I don't know where my lover's face has gone,
But the green waves roll eastward, the same as always.

———————————

清平樂

金風細細，
葉葉梧桐墜。
綠酒初嘗人易醉，
一枕小窗濃睡。

紫薇朱槿花殘，
斜陽卻照闌干。
雙燕欲歸時節，
銀屏昨夜微寒。

Ti the air o *LOWN PLEISURS*[13]

The hairst wind reishle-reishles,
Ti ilka plane-tree leaf's whummlt;
Guid drink'll easy get a bodie fou at the first preein,
Sae it'll be a bowster ablow the wee winnock,
  ti sleep soun as a horn.

Purpie myrtle an reid rose[14] dwyne,
A sklentin sun lichts the palins;
This is the time swallas think to win awa in twaesomes,
Yestreen, a garb o rime on the siller hallans.

---

13 Highly Commended, Scots Language Society *Sangschaw* competition, 2021.
14 Strictly speaking, the China Rose, Hibiscus rosa-sinensis L.

To the air of *QUIET PLEASURES*

The autumn wind whistles and whistles,
Till every sycamore leaf is blown down;
Good liquor will easily get you drunk at the first tasting,
So it'll be the bolster below the little window,
     to sleep like a log.

Purple myrtle and red rose fade,
A slanting sun lights the fence;
This is the time swallows think to go away in pairs,
Last night, a touch of frost on the silver screens.

———————

木蘭花

池塘水綠風微暖，
記得玉真初見面。
重頭歌韻響琤琮，
入破舞腰紅亂旋。

玉鈎闌下香階畔。
醉後不知斜日晚。
當時共我賞花人，
點檢如今無一半。

Ti the air o *MAGNOLIA FLOURISH*

A wee waff o warm wind owre the green watter o the stank,
An A mind the first time A saw ma bonnie jo;
The claitterin lilt o the double-heidit ballant verses,
The fankle o dancers birlin reid at the ongang o the eik.

Palace steppie-stairs ablow jowelt quarter-mune palins,
Eftir our dram we niver saw the sklentin sun set;
Somebodie lou'd the flouers alang wi me langsyne,
But A see nou she's no the hauf o whit yince she wis.

To the air of *MAGNOLIA BLOSSOM*

A small gust of warm wind over the green water of the pool,
And I remember the first time I saw my fine lover;
The clattering rhythm of the double-headed ballad verses,
The knots of dancers spinning in red at the entry to the coda.

Palace steps below jewelled quarter-moon palings,
After our drinks we never saw the slanting sun set;
Somebody loved the flowers alongside me long ago,
But now I see she's not half what once she was.

———————————

木蘭花

燕鴻過後鶯歸去，
細算浮生千萬緒。
長於春夢幾多時，
散似秋雲無覓處。

聞琴解佩神仙侶，
挽斷羅衣留不住。
勸君莫作獨醒人，
爛醉花間應有數。

Ti the air o *MAGNOLIA FLOURISH*

Nou geese an swans are gane an yalla-yites wan awa,
Consider yir bruckle life an aa its monie cares:
Ye grew up in a dream o spring – an hou lang did it lest?
It skailt like the clouds o hairst-time, nae mair ti be socht.

A guid-neibour-like jo'll lissen ti the clarsach
    an gie awa her jowels,[15]
An tho ye ryvit yir sleeves o gauze, ye wadnae cud kep her:
A bid ye, guidsir, dinna be a bodie at wakes his leelane,
For weirdit ye be to get roarin fou mang the flouers.

---

15 While the 琴 qin is organologically distinct from the clarsach, in their own time
both were prestige string instruments played by aristocrats and intellectuals. This
little poem is heavily freighted with allusions and quotations. *Spring* also has strong
erotic associations.

YAN SHU

To the air of *MAGNOLIA BLOSSOM*

Now geese and swans are gone and orioles away,
Consider your uncertain life and all its many cares:
You grew up in a dream of spring – and how long did it last?
It scattered like the clouds of autumn, nowhere to be sought.

An elven-like love will listen to your zither
    and give away her jewels,
But though you tore your fancy gauze sleeves,
    you couldn't keep her:
I bid you, sir, don't be someone who wakes alone,
For fated you are to get rotten drunk among the flowers.

木蘭花

綠楊芳草長亭路，
年少拋人容易去。
樓頭殘夢五更鐘，
花底離愁三月雨。

無情不似多情苦，
一寸還成千萬縷。
天涯地角有窮時，
只有相思無盡處。

Ti the air o *MAGNOLIA FLOURISH*

Green sauchs an sweet gress on the road
    ti the lang chynge-hous,
It wis easy then for a younker like me to forhoo ma jo
    an win awa;
Bruckle's ma dreams in the laft at the dawin bell,
The sorra o twynin, ablow the flouers,
    in the third month's rain.

Nae luve is sair, but owre muckle luve's sairer,
An inch o't turns ti a million raivelt sorras;
In time the lift's en an the heel o the yirth'll
    baith be forspent,
An this luve alane'll ne'er devaul.[16]

---

16 Highly commended, Scots Language Society *Sangschaw* competition, 2021.

To the air of *MAGNOLIA BLOSSOM*

Green willow and sweet grass on the road
    to the long post-house,
It was easy then for a youngster like me to forsake my lover
    and go away;
Fragile are my dreams in the tower at the dawn bell,
The sorrow of separation, below the flowers,
    in the third month rain.

No love hurts, but too much love hurts even more,
An inch of it turns into a million tangled sorrows;
In time the sky's end and the heel of the earth will
    both be spent,
And only this love will never end.

———————————

踏莎行

祖席離歌，
長亭別宴，
香塵已隔猶回面。
居人匹馬映林嘶，
行人去棹依波轉。

畫閣魂消，
高樓目斷，
斜陽只送平波遠。
無窮無盡是離愁，
天涯地角尋思遍。

Ti the air o *STRAMPIN OWRE SEGGS*

A pairtin gless, a sang o twynin,
A fareweill foy at the lang chynge-hous;
A'm lookin back yit, tho A'm lang past the perfumit mools.
Ma jo's pownie nichers in the sheddae o the shaws,
An here's me, the traivler, awa wi the lilt o oars on the swaws.

Ma sowl eelies awa in the pentit laft,
Frae the hie touer A can look nae mair;
A sklentin sun hyne awa convoys the level swaws.
Niver nae en, niver nae devaul ti thae sorras o sinderin,
Ti the lift's en, ti the heel o the yirth,
  this hairt-hunger ye'll fin.

To the air of *TRAMPING OVER SEDGE*

A parting glass, a song of leaving,
A farewell party at the long post-house;
I look behind me still, though I'm long past the fragrant soil.
My love's pony neighs in the shade of the woods,
And here I am, the traveller,
      away with the beat of oars on the waves.

My soul slips away in the painted loft,
From the high tower I can look no more;
A slanting sun far away convoys the even waves.
Never an end, never a rest from these sorrows of separation,
To the sky's end, to the heel of the earth,
      you'll find this yearning everywhere.

———————

踏莎行

小徑紅稀，
芳郊綠遍，
高臺樹色陰陰見。
春風不解禁楊花，
濛濛亂撲行人面。

翠葉藏鶯，
朱簾隔燕，
爐香靜逐游絲轉。
一場愁夢酒醒時，
斜陽卻照深深院。

Ti the air o *STRAMPIN OWRE SEGGS*

Few the reid petals on the wee path,
But aagates are douce green outlans,
An mirk's the sheddas o the trees fornent the hie laft;
Spring winds can neither haud nor bind the sauch tossels,
That tirlin an flichterin skite pell-mell at the traivler's face

Mang emerant leafs dern yalla-yites,
Yont crammasy hingers there's swallas,
The saft reek o the incense burner chases the waggin wobs;
An aye the yin wearifu dream whan the drink weirs aff,
As sklentin sun shines deep an deep inti the back-court.

To the air of *TRAMPING OVER SEDGE*

Few the red petals on the little path,
But everywhere are sweet green suburbs,
And dark's the shadows of the trees in front of the high loft;
Spring winds can neither hold nor bind the willow catkins,
That whirling and fluttering slap pell-mell
     at the traveller's face

Among emerald leaves hide orioles,
Beyond crimson curtains there's swallows,
The soft smoke of the incense burner
     chases the wagging spiderwebs;
And always the one weary dream when the drink wears off,
As slanting sun shines deep and deep into the courtyard.

———————————

踏莎行

碧海無波，
瑤臺有路。
思量便合雙飛去。
當時輕別意中人，
山長水遠知何處。

綺席凝塵，
香閨掩霧。
紅箋小字憑誰附。
高樓目盡欲黃昏，
梧桐葉上蕭蕭雨。

Ti the air o *STRAMPIN OWRE SEGGS*

Nae swaws on the blue sea,
But there's a road ti the Jowelt Terrace;
In thocht we wad flee there as a twaesome;
Back then sae lichtlie did A pairt wi him that's in ma hairt,
But nou lang's the hills, fer's the watters,
     an A kenna whaur he'll be.

The pearlin rugs are thick wi stour
The weimens' bouer's happit in rouk,
Wee words on reid letter-paper,
     whae can A get ti convoy them?
Frae the hie touer A look ferawa, ettlin for the lang gloamin,
An rain smirr-smirrs on plane tree leafs.

To the air of *TRAMPING OVER SEDGE*

No waves on the blue sea,
But there's a road to the Jewelled Terrace;
In thought we'd fly there as a couple;
Back then so lightly did I part with him that's in my heart,
But now long are the hills, far the waters,
     and I don't know where he'll be.

The embroidered rugs are thick with dust
The women's bower deep in mist,
Small words on red letter-paper, who can I get to send them?
From the high tower I look far away, eager for the long dusk,
And rain drizzles on the sycamore leaves.

———————————

蝶戀花

六曲闌干偎碧樹，
楊柳風輕，
展盡黃金縷。
誰把鈿箏移玉柱，
穿簾海燕雙飛去。

滿眼游絲兼落絮，
紅杏開時，
一霎清明雨。
濃睡覺來鶯亂語，
驚殘好夢無尋處。

Ti the air o *BUTTERFLEES LOU FLOUERS*

Emerant trees hing owre the sax-bou palins,
Licht's the wind throu the sauchs
That rax out their gowden tossels,
But wha'll fettle the inlaid zither-trees?
Throu the hingers sea-swallas in twaesomes flee.

Aawhaur A look A see maggie-wabs an sauch-palmies,
But whan the reid abricos flourish,
The Day o the Deid rains instanter will come.
A sleep soun as a peerie an wauken ti the yalla-yites' yatter,
The gliff A get spyles the bonnie dream A'll finnd nae mair.

To the air of *BUTTERFLIES LOVE FLOWERS*

Emerald trees hang over the six-bend railings,
Light is the wind through the willows
That reach out their golden tassels,
But who will put the inlaid zither-bridges right?
Through the blinds petrels in couples fly.

Everywhere I look I see gossamer and willow catkins,
But when the red apricots bloom,
The Day of the Dead rains will instantly come.
I sleep sound as a top and waken to the orioles' chatter,
The surprise I get spoils the lovely dream I'll find no more.

———————————

韓縝
HAN ZHEN (1019-1097)

A lesser-known poet, he gained his *Jinshi* degree in 1049, and served in the Transport Commission and the Bureau of Military Affairs, before promotion to Vice Director of the Imperial Secretariat. He also served as magistrate in Yingchangfu, now Xuchang, Henan Province.

鳳簫吟

鎖離愁
連綿無際,
來時陌上初燻,
繡幃人念遠,
暗垂珠露,
泣送征輪。
長行長在眼,
更重重、
遠水孤雲。
但望極樓高,
盡日目斷王孫。

消魂,
池塘別後,
曾行處、
綠妒輕裙。
恁時攜素手,
亂花飛絮裏,
緩步香茵。
朱顏空自改,
向年年、
芳意長新。
遍綠野,
嬉遊醉眼,
莫負青春。

Ti the air o *BALLANT O THE PHENIX WHISTLE*

Sneckit up wi the sorra o sinderin,
Even-on an enless,
Tho sweet wis the first saur o the bauks whan A cam,
Inwith browderie bed-hingers a bodie micht think on him
    at's fer awa;
In hidlins lettin tears faa like pearls,
Greetin, A convoyed the traivlin chairriot.
The lang road's aye in ma ee,
Doublt an mair doublt,
Ferawa watters an the yae cloud its lane:
In vain A leuk, as fer as A can see,
    the leelang day in my hie touer,
But ma prince is sindert frae ma sicht.

Ma sowl's eeliet awa,
Sin bi the pule we pairtit,
Whaur yince we walkt,
An the gress invyit ma flindrikin skirt;
A mind on the times ye tuik ma white haun
Mang a guddle o flouers an flichterin sauch palmies,
As slaw we steppit owre the sweet meedies.
Ma rosie cheek's a wee thing chyngit
As years an years gaed by,
But yir kind love is aye new:
As aagates in the green landart airts
Whaur ye sport an play wi tosie een,
Dinna let the springtime o yir youthheid misgae.

To the air of
BALLAD OF THE PHOENIX WHISTLE

Locked up with the sorrow of parting,
Unbroken and endless,
Though sweet was the first savour of the garden paths
    when I came,
Inside embroidered bed-curtains
    someone might think on him that's far away;
In secret letting tears like pearls fall,
Weeping, I accompanied the traveling chariot.
The long road's still in my eye,
Doubled and doubled again,
Faraway waters and a single cloud on its own:
In vain I look, as far as I can see,
    the entire day in my high tower,
But my own prince is sundered from my sight.

My soul has slipped away,
Since by the pool we parted,
Where once we walked,
And the grass envied my flimsy skirt;
I remember the times you took my white hand
Among a mess of flowers and fluttering willow catkins,
As slowly we stepped across the sweet meadows.
My rosy cheek has changed
As years and years have gone by,
But your kind love is always new:
As all over the green countryside
Where you sport and play with tipsy eyes,
Don't let the springtime of your youth miscarry.

———————

宋祁
SONG QI (998-1061)

A noted poet, famous historian, and, with Ouyang Xiu, author of the official *New Tang History* (1060): he was placed top of the list when he and his brother both took the civil service examinations in 1023, but protocol forced him to yield that place to his older brother. He held many high-ranking positions, and his poetry made him famous, to the extent that he was nicknamed "Prime Minister Red Apricot" after one line of this, his most famous poem, the only one in *300 Song Ci*.

木蘭花

東城漸覺風光好，
縠皺波紋迎客棹。
綠楊煙外曉雲輕，
紅杏枝頭春意鬧。

浮生長恨歡娛少，
肯愛千金輕一笑？
為君持酒勸斜陽，
且向花間留晚照。

Ti the air o *MAGNOLIA FLOURISH*

The scenery at the Eastren Waa's braw gettin,
Swaws like bumflt silk on the watter walcome outlan cobles;
Green sauchs an the smaa clouds o dawin yont the rouk:
Springtime's aa stushie an stour on reid abrico beuchs.

A rue this gangrel life that hesna brocht muckle fun,
Aye owre willin ti lou siller or lichtlie a bonnie smile;
But A'll raise a gless ti ye, sir, an threip at the sklentin sun
    ti bide a wee,
Ti kep mang the flouers the last glisk o the gloamin.

To the air of *MAGNOLIA BLOSSOM*

The scenery at the Eastern Wall's getting beautiful,
Waves like rumpled silk on the water welcome
    visiting rowing boats;
Green willows and the small clouds of dawn beyond the mist:
Springtime's all bustle and rush on red apricot boughs.

I rue this drifting life that hasn't brought me that much fun,
Always too ready to love money or scorn a bonny smile;
But I'll raise a glass to you, sir, and beg the slanting sun
    to stay a bit,
To keep among the flowers the last gleam of the gloaming.

———————

歐陽修
OUYANG XIU (1007-1072)

One of the most remarkable men of the age, a highly successful civil service career gave him time to write, as historian, literary critic, pioneering epigrapher, creator of the new genre of *shihua* "chats on poetry", widely admired essayist, and poet. His gently erotic and quietly humorous love poems, while not ground-breaking in theme or form, are natural and very readable.

採桑子

群芳過後西湖好，
狼籍殘紅，
飛絮濛濛，
垂柳闌干盡日風。

笙歌散盡遊人去，
始覺春空，
垂下簾櫳，
雙燕歸來細雨中。

Ti the air o *PICKIN BLAEBERRIES*[17]

Yince the time o flouers is by, Wastlin Loch is bonniest,
A slaister an soss o reid petals,
A smirr-smirr o fleein palmies,
Willie-wands hingin owre palins in the wind.

Moothies[18] an singin aa dune an towrists skailt,
A stert ti feel that springtime's tuim;
A lat the hingers doun,
As twaesomes o swallas come hame in the smaa smaa rain.

---

17 Naturalised. The original has mulberries.
18 The shēng 笙 is a mouth-blown free-reed instrument of great antiquity, which long predates and probably inspired the harmonica: a French Jesuit first brought one to Europe in the late 18th century.

To the air of *PICKING MULBERRIES*

Once the time of flowers has passed, West Lake is best,
A confusion of red petals,
Flying catkins in a fine drizzle,
Willow branches hanging over fences in the wind.

Mouth-organs and singing finished and tourists scattered,
I start to feel how empty the springtime is;
I let the blinds down,
As pairs of swallows come home in the fine rain.

訴衷情

清晨簾幕卷輕霜，
呵手試梅妝。
都緣自有離恨，
故畫作遠山長。

思往事，
惜流芳，
易成傷。
擬歌先斂，
欲笑還顰，
最斷人腸。

Ti the air o *SPEAK YIR MIND*

The hingers wir rowed up in the smaa hours
    wi cranreuch on them,
She wis blawin on her fingers ti fettle her paintrie;
She wis hairt-sair at our sinderin,
Sae she pentit her brous
Lang an hie as the ferawa hills.

Thinkin nou on times bypast,
A rue for days langsyne,
An A easy get mistempert;
She'd haud back first, afore she sang,
Gaun ti smile, she'd froun insteid:
Thon's whit breks a hairt maist o aa.

To the air of *SPEAK YOUR MIND*

The blinds were rolled up in the small hours
    with frost on them,
She was blowing on her fingers to fix her make-up;
All heart-sore at our parting,
She painted her brows
Long and high as the faraway hills.

Thinking now on times past,
I rue for days long ago,
And easily get ill-tempered;
She'd hold back first, before she sang,
Going to smile, she'd frown instead:
That's what breaks a heart most of all.

———————

踏莎行

候館梅殘，
溪橋柳細，
草薰風暖搖征轡。
離愁漸遠漸無窮，
迢迢不斷如春水。

寸寸柔腸，
盈盈粉淚，
樓高莫近危闌倚。
平蕪盡處是春山，
行人更在春山外。

Ti the air o *STRAMPIN OWRE SEGGS*

Dwynin's the ploum flourish at the watchie-touer,
Nesh an fine the willie-wands,
The gress is sweet, the wind blaws warm owre
     airmy branks an saiddles;
The sorra o pairtin, the faurer awa the mair desparit,
Hyne, hyne-awa, aye an on, like the spring spates.

Ilka inch o a saft hairt,
Full een, tears on pouther:
Hie's the touer, sae dinna you hing owre near the palins;
The gerss-lan meedies rin the lenth o the spring hills,
But yir traivler's ayont thae green spring hills again.

To the air of *TRAMPING OVER SEDGE*

Failing is the plum blossom at the watchtower,
Tender and fine the willow twigs,
The grass is sweet, the wind blows warm over
    army bridles and saddles;
The sorrow of parting, the further away the more desperate,
Far, far away, and ever and on, like the spring floods.

Every inch of a soft heart,
Full eyes, tears on powder:
High's the tower, so don't you lean too near the railing;
The grassland meadows run as the length of
    the spring hills,
But your traveller is beyond the green spring hills again.

———————————

蝶戀花

庭院深深深幾許?
楊柳堆煙,
簾幕無重數。
玉勒雕鞍遊冶處,
樓高不見章臺路。

雨橫風狂三月暮,
門掩黃昏,
無計留春住。
淚眼問花花不語,
亂紅飛過鞦韆去。

Ti the air o *BUTTERFLEES LOU FLOUERS*

Deep an deep's baith court an haa, but hou deep?
Hie-heapit rouks mang sauchs an poplars,
Like hingers o silk, gang upon gang;
A ride around wi jowelt branks an fantoosh saiddle,
The houses that hie, A canna fin Bordel Raw.

Flatlins skiffs the rain in the blast o a third month at e'en,
Yetts steikit in the gloamin,
But nae wey they'll kep the spring;
A speir at the flouers wi a tear in ma ee but they sae naethin,
They flee flichterin reid, past the shuggie-shoo.

To the air of *BUTTERFLIES LOVE FLOWERS*

Deep and deep are both court and hall, but how deep?
High-heaping mist among willows and poplars,
Like curtains of silk, layer upon layer;
I ride around with jewelled bridle and fancy saddle,
The houses so high, I can't find Brothel Row.

Horizontal the rain in the blast of a third month evening,
Gates shut in the twilight,
But no way they'll make the spring stay;
With tears in my eyes I ask the flowers but they don't speak,
Flickering red, they fly past the swing.

———————

蝶戀花

誰道閒情拋棄久？
每到春來，
惆悵還依舊。
日日花前常病酒，
不辭鏡裏朱顏瘦。

河畔青蕪堤上柳，
為問新愁，
何事年年有？
獨立小橋風滿袖，
平林新月人歸後。

Ti the air o *BUTTERFLEES LOU FLOUERS*

Wha says youthheid's luve in idleset can be lang forhooiet?
Whene'er springtime comes in,
A'm as dowie an wae as A wis afore;
Day an daily A'm fou forenent the flouers,
An in the gless ma rosie cheek's shilpit, A'll no nae-say't.

Green gress on the haugh, sauchs on the dam,
A speir at them anent my new care:
Hou come year eftir year it's aye there?
Staunin ma lane on the wee brig, the wind fills ma sleeves,
A new moon wis owre the level shaw eftir a bodie won hame.

To the air of *BUTTERFLIES LOVE FLOWERS*

Who says youth's love in idleness can be forsaken for long?
Whenever springtime comes in,
I'm as sad and woeful as I was before;
Day in and day out I'm sozzled by the flowers,
And in the mirror my rosy cheek's shrunken and drawn,
    I won't deny.

Green grass on the riverbank, willows on the dam,
I ask them about my new sorrow:
How come year after year it's still there?
Standing alone on the little bridge, the wind fills my sleeves,
A new moon was above the level woods
    when someone went home.

———————————

蝶戀花

幾日行雲何處去？
忘了歸來，
不道春將暮。
百草千花寒食路，
香車繫在誰家樹？

淚眼倚樓頻獨語，
雙燕來時，
陌上相逢否？
撩亂春愁如柳絮，
依依夢裏無尋處。

Ti the air o *BUTTERFLEES LOU FLOUERS*

Hou monie days sin ye gaed kens-whaurawa
    like the driven cairry?
Ye forgot ti come hame,
An dinna ken spring's nearhaun by;
Hunners o gresses, thousans o flouers
    on the Cauld Mait Day roads,[19]
But whae's tree is yir braw powny an trap tethert ti nou?

A hing on the touer wi a tear in ma ee, rame-ramin ti masel,
"Gin a pair o swallaes comes thegither,
Will we forgaither on the roadie?"
Spring sorra's steirit up like tossels on the sauchs:
Sweirt A am ti lea a dream A'll ne'er fin mair.

---

19 The day before Qingming (The Day o the Deid) in early April, when cooking is
forbidden.

To the air of *BUTTERFLIES LOVE FLOWERS*

How many days since like driven clouds
    you went who knows where?
You forgot to come home,
And don't know spring's near at hand;
Hundreds of grasses, thousands of flowers
    on the Cold Food Day roads,
But whose tree is your fine pony and trap tethered to now?

I lean on the tower with tears in my eyes, repeating to myself,
"If a pair of swallows come together,
Will we meet on the garden path?"
Spring sorrow is stirred up like catkins on the willows:
I'm not willing to leave a dream I'll never find again.

———————

木蘭花

別後不知君遠近，
觸目淒涼多少悶！
漸行漸遠漸無書，
水闊魚沉何處問？

夜深風竹敲秋韻，
萬葉千聲皆是恨。
故欹單枕夢中尋，
夢又不成燈又燼。

Ti the air o *MAGNOLIA FLOURISH*

Eftir ye gaed A kentna wir ye near or fer, sir,
A'm that disjaskit, aa A see's dreich to me;
The langer A traivel, the less yir letters,
The watter's wide an the fishes are dernt,
     sae whaur cud A speir?

In deep nicht the bamboo dirlin in the wind's
     the soun o hairst time,
Reishlin leafs bi the thousans aa soun like the rue;
Sae A lie on ma lanesome bowster, ettlin ti seek ye in dreams,
But the dreams arena feckfu, an the caunle's aiss.

To the air of *MAGNOLIA BLOSSOM*

After you went I didn't know if you were near or far, sir,
I'm so dejected, all I see is dull and depressing to me;
The longer I travel, the fewer your letters,
The water is wide and the fish hidden, so where could I ask?

In deep night the bamboo rattling in the wind
    is the sound of autumn,
Rustling leaves by the thousand all sounding like regret;
So I lie on my lonely pillow, trying to seek you in dreams,
But the dreams don't come true, and the candle's ash.

———————

臨江仙

柳外輕雷池上雨，
雨聲滴碎荷聲。
小樓西角斷虹明。
闌干倚處，
待得月華生。

燕子飛來窺畫棟，
玉鉤垂下簾旌。
涼波不動簟紋平。
水精雙枕，
傍有墮釵橫。

Ti the air o *WATTERSIDE TRANSCENDANDS*

Saft thunder ayont the sauchs, rain on the stank,
Rain draps plink-plinkin on the lotus leafs;
Bricht's the watergaw horn at the touer's western neuk;
Here whaur A hing on the palins,
Waitin on the mune risin in glore.

Swallas come fleein ti keek frae the pentit riggin-trees,
Hingers let doun frae heuks o jade;
The caller swaws are still as the sett on ma bamboo mat;
Aside twa crystal bowsters,[20]
A faan-doun hairprein o gowd.

---

20 Traditionally, Chinese people slept on headrests, rather than pillows. These were
often ceramic, metal, or wooden, though sometimes covered with soft fabrics: this
seems to refer to ones of glass, which would be cool in the hot nights of sum-
mer.

To the air of *RIVERSIDE TRANSCENDANTS*

Soft thunder beyond the willows, rain on the pond,
Rain drops tinkle on the lotus leaves;
Bright is the rainbow's horn at the tower's western corner,
Here where I lean on the railing,
Waiting for the moon to rise in glory.

Swallows come flying to peek from the painted roofbeams,
Blinds are let down from hooks of jade;
The cool waves are still as the pattern on my bamboo mat;
Beside two crystal headrests,
A fallen hairpin of gold.

浣溪沙

堤上游人逐畫船，
拍堤春水四垂天。
綠楊樓外出鞦韆。

白髮戴花君莫笑，
六幺催拍盞頻傳。
人生何處似樽前！

Ti the air o *WESHIN BURNIE SAUNS*

On the dam towrist folk an pentit cobles hae aa wan awa;
Spring watter lapperin at the dam is colourt like the lift;
Ablow the touer mang green sauchs
    a shuggie-shoo heaves abune the waa.

The'r a flouer in his white pow – dinna lauch, sirs:
The lilt o the Wee Sixes dance is eggin him on,
    an the bickers are birlin;
Whaur wad we be in this life athout a dram afore us?

To the air of *WASHING STREAMLET SANDS*

On the dam tourists and painted rowing boats
    have all gone away;
Spring water lapping at the dam is coloured like the sky;
Below the tower among green willows
    a swing heaves above the wall.

There's a flower in his white hair – don't laugh, sirs:
The rhythm of the Little Sixes dance is egging him on,
    and the glasses come thick and fast;
Where would we be in this life without a dram before us?

———

浪淘沙

把酒祝東風，
且共從容。
垂楊紫陌洛城東，
總是當時攜手處，
游遍芳叢。

聚散苦匆匆，
此恨無窮。
今年花勝去年紅，
可惜明年花更好，
知與誰同？

Ti the air o *SAUN CAIRRIED BI THE SWAW*

Raise a gless an bid the eastern wind come in,
An tak yir ease wi me, eh?
Weepie-willies purpie the path east o Rinwatter Toun,[21]
Whaur aye in times bypast we'd jyne hauns,
An dauner roun amang the bonnie flouers.

Meetins an pairtins flee by sairlie quick,
But this rue's niver-endin;
This year's flouers are reider nor fernyear's,
An the peety o't is, neist year's 'll be better yit:
Kens whae we'll be wi then...

---

21 i.e. Luoyang. See n.4 above.

To the air of *SAND CARRIED BY THE WAVE*

Raise a glass and bid the east wind come in,
And take your ease with me, eh?
Weeping willows purple the path east of Runwater Town,
Where always in times past we'd join hands,
And wander round among the pretty flowers.

Meetings and partings fly by painfully quick,
But this regret is never-ending;
This year's flowers are redder than last year's,
And the pity of it is, next year's will be better yet:
Who knows who we'll be with then...

青玉案

一年春事都來幾，
早過了、三之二。
綠暗紅嫣渾可事，
綠楊庭院，
暖風簾幕，
有個人憔悴。

買花載酒長安市，
又爭似家山見桃李？
不枉東風吹客淚，
相思難表，
夢魂無據，
惟有歸來是。

Ti the air o *BROD O GREEN JADE*

Hou monie times in yin year will spring come?
It's owre sune by, twa-pairt out o thrie nou;
Fine an cannie baith, the derk greens an skyrie reids:
Green sauchs in the back-court,
A warm wind throu the hingers,
But the'r yin bodie that's vext an pale an wan.

Sellin flouers or outsettin drink in Langpeace Toun,[22]
Hou wad that compare wi seein peach an ploum flourish
    on the hills o hame?
Nae wunner the eastren wind blaws on an incomer's tears,
Luve's a seikness that's ill to tell,
Bieldless the dreamin sowl,
Winnin hame's the yae an yin richt thing nou.

---

22 i.e. the capital at Chang'an, now Xi'an, in Shaanxi Province.

To the air of *BOARD OF GREEN JADE*

How many times in a single year will spring come?
It's gone too soon, and two-parts out of three now;
Fine and pleasant both, the dark greens and bright reds:
Green willows in the back courtyard,
A warm wind through the blinds,
But there's one that's vexed and pale and wan.

Selling flowers or serving drinks in Langpeace Toun,
How would that compare with seeing peach
    and plum blossom on the hills of home?
No wonder the east wind blows on a stranger's tears,
Love's an illness that's hard to tell,
Unfixed and shelterless the dreaming soul,
Going home's the one and only right thing now.

聂冠卿
NIE GUANQING (988-1042)

Nie was born in Anhui Province, and little of his work has sur-
vived. He served in the Imperial Library, was sent as an envoy
to the Khitan nomads of NE Asia, and a year before his death
at 55, he was promoted to the Hanlin Academy. The only poem
of his selected for *300 Song Ci* has been praised for its techni-
cal deftness and richness of emotional response.

多丽

想人生，
美景良辰堪惜。
问其间、
赏心乐事，
就中难是并得。
况东城、
风台沙苑，
泛晴波、
浅照金碧。
露洗华桐，
烟霏丝柳，
绿阴摇曳，
荡春一色。
画堂迥、
玉簪琼佩，
高会尽词客。
清欢久、

重然绛蜡，
别就瑶席。
有翩若轻鸿体态，
暮为行雨标格。
逞朱唇、
缓歌妖丽，
似听流莺乱花隔。
慢舞萦回，
娇鬟低亸，
腰肢纤细困无力。
忍分散、
彩云归后，
何处更寻觅。
休辞醉，
明月好花，
莫谩轻掷。

Ti the air o *WHIT BONNIE*

Think on this life,
Bonnie scenery an braw days are warth treisurin,
For amang them aa
We'll can tak our pleisur an be gled:
Sin auld langsyne it hesna been easy ti hae baith.
Mairatowre in the Eastren Toun[23]
In Sandyburn Gairdens at the Phenix Terrace
Braid caller swaws
Refleckin gowd an green,
Dew weshes planetree flourish,
Rouks hing on willie-wands,
Green sheddaes shoogle in the wind,
An it's aa the colours o enless spring.
Ti the Haa o Paintrie they win back,
Wi their hairpreins o jade an jowelt pendies,
An ilka makar's at their hie-bendit pairties:
Lang's their fine ballants,
Crammasy caunles kinnelt owre an owre –
Then they're awa ti anither fantoosh foy.
They cairry theirsels like sterty swans about ti flee awa,
They're like the rainy cairry at een,
Shawin aff reid lips,
In the glamourie o their slaw sangs,
Like lissenin ti yalla-yites snoove amang the flouers,
Weavin in an out in a houlie dance,
Their bonnie hair danglin doun in plaits,
Tho jimp's their middles,
An fushionless they seem.

---

23 In the suburbs of Chang'an, now Xi'an, in Shaanxi Province.

Pairtins an twynins they'll thole,
An yince the bonnie clouds win awa,
Whaur wad a bodie e'er fin them again?
Dinna you nae-say a bevvy,
Bricht munes or bonnie flouers:
Dinna thraw yir youthheid awa sae easy.

To the air of *HOW PRETTY*

Think about this life,
Lovely scenery and beautiful days are worth cherishing,
For among them all
We can take our pleasure and be glad:
Since long ago it's not been easy to have both.
Moreover in the Eastern Town
In Sandyburn Gardens at the Phoenix Terrace
Broad fresh waves
Reflect the golden and the green,
Dew washes planetree blossoms,
Mists hang on willow wands,
Green shadows shaking in the wind,
And it's all the colours of endless spring.
To the Hall of Painting they return,
With their hairpins of jade and jewelled pendants,
And every poet's at their posh parties:
Long are their fine ballads,
Crimson candles kindled over and over –
Then they're off to another fancy social event.
They carry themselves like startled swans flying off,
They're like the rainy sky at dusk,
Showing off red lips,
In the magic of their slow songs,
Like listening to orioles glide among the flowers,
Weaving in and out in a measured dance,
Their lovely hair dangling down in plaits,
Though slim are their waists,
And weak and fragile they seem.
Partings and sunderings they'll bear,
And once the lovely clouds have gone,

Where would someone ever find them again?
Don't say no to a drink,
To bright moons or pretty flowers:
Don't throw your youth away so easily.

———————

柳永
LIU YONG (987-1053)

A famous poet and musician, he finally passed the *Jinshi* examination at the age of 47 after many failed attempts, and was appointed as a magistrate in Zhejiang Province. As a young man he spent his time in the entertainment quarter of the capital, and was much admired by singing-girls. He was a pioneer in introducing the long-form *manci* ("slow lyrics") which allowed more room to develop new topics, bringing him great fame and popularity, but his mixture of literary and colloquial language was controversial, even though it was balanced and expressive.

曲玉管

隴首雲飛，
江邊日晚，
煙波滿目憑闌久。
立望關河蕭索，
千里清秋。
忍凝眸。
杳杳神京，
盈盈仙子，
別來錦字終難偶。
斷雁無憑，
冉冉飛下汀洲。
思悠悠。
暗想當初，
有多少、
幽歡佳會，
豈知聚散難期，
翻成雨恨雲愁。
阻追遊。
每登山臨水，
惹起平生心事，
一場消黯，
永日無言，
卻下層樓。

Ti the air o *BOWIT JADE SHAWM*

Fleein clouds on the hill heids,
Late sun on the haughs,
Drowie swaws fill ma een as lang A hing on the raivlin;
Aa A see's a dreich land o desolation:
A thousan mile o caller hairst-time
An A canna thole the sicht o't.
Mirk, mirk's the Halie Muckle Toun[24],
Bonnie, bonnie's the Transcendand lasses,
Braw as brocades, an A'll ne'er see them mair;
A tint guse hes nane ti lippen til,
Houlie an slaw it flees doun ti the annay,
An dowie, dowie, it thinks lang.
In dern A mind aathing bygane,
Hou monie lown times, blithe times, an soirees –
Whae kent meetins an twynins cudna be foreseen,
Afore they turnt ti the sorras o clouds an rues o rain?
Taiglt wi follaein the thrang o towrists,
Ilka time A sclim a hill or come ti a watter,
It steirs up aathing A've ettlt at for a lifetime,
Then it's aa derk, an gane:
No the ae word the haill leelang day,
Sae back doun the stair A gang.

---

24 i.e. Chang'an, now Xi'an, or Langpeace Toun, the capital city of 11 dynasties.

To the air of *BENT JADE SHAWM*

Flying clouds on the hilltops,
Late sun on the riverbanks,
Misty waves fill my eyes as I lean long on the railing;
All I see is a dreary land of desolation:
A thousand miles of refreshing autumn
And I can't bear the sight of it.
Dark, dark's the Holy City,
Bonny, bonny the transcendent lasses,
Beautiful as brocades, and I'll never see them again;
A lost goose has no one to rely on,
Leisurely and slow it flies down to the river island,
And dolefully, dolefully it thinks on.
In secret I recall all the past,
How many peaceful times, happy times, and parties –
Who knew meetings and partings would be unforeseeable,
Before they turned into the sorrows of clouds
        and the regrets of rain?
Weary of following a throng of tourists,
Each time I climb a hill or go near a river,
It stirs up everything I've aimed at for a lifetime,
Then it's all dark, and gone:
Not a single word the whole long day,
So back down the stairs I go.

———————

雨霖铃

寒蟬悽切，
對長亭晚，
驟雨初歇。
都門帳飲無緒，
留戀處，
蘭舟催發。
執手相看淚眼，
竟無語凝噎。
念去去，
千里煙波，
暮靄沉沉楚天闊。

多情自古傷離別，
更那堪冷落清秋節！
今宵酒醒何處？
楊柳岸，
曉風殘月。
此去經年，
應是良辰好景虛設。
便縱有千種風情，
更與何人說？

Ti the air o *BELLS IN THE ONDING*

The dowie drone o chairkers in the cauld,
In the gloamin forenent the lang chynge-hous,
An a shouer o rain juist new devault;
Wi fankelt hairt she pit on a foy at the Capital Port,
Juist ti byde there wi her lovie,
But clamant wis the wee coble ti set out;
We held hauns, lookit in ilkither's begrutten een,
In the en, nae words, but thrappelt tears;
Thinkin on yon lang lang road,
A thousan mile o faemin swaws,
An blin, blin rouks owre the braid southron lift.

Sin auld langsyne, feelin fowk hae suffert at pairtins,
But A can thole this hairtless caller hairst-time nae mair:
Whan A sober up this nicht, whit'll it be?
Watterside sauchs?
A dwynin mune? Dawin winds?
This wa-gaun'll be for years;
It sud be a happy day,
But the bonnie scenery's nae uise.
Gin A e'er hed a thousan smert-like lovies
Whae o them cud A tell?

To the air of *BELLS IN HEAVY RAIN*

The doleful drone of cicadas in the cold,
In the twilight in front of the long change-house,
And a shower of rain just newly stopped;
With troubled heart she put on a farewell party
    at the Capital Gate,
Just to abide there with her lover,
But insistent was the small boat to set out;
We held hands, looked in each other's tear-filled eyes,
In the end, no words, but tears choked back;
Thinking of that long, long road,
A thousand miles of foaming billows,
And blind, blind fogs across the broad southern skies.

Since ancient times, feeling people have suffered at partings,
But I can endure this heartless cool autumn no more:
When I sober up tonight, what will it be?
Waterside willows?
A fading moon? Dawn winds?
This going away will be for years;
It should be a happy day,
But the lovely scenery's no use.
If I ever had a thousand stylish lovers
Which of them could I tell?

蝶戀花

佇倚危樓風細細。
望極春愁,
黯黯生天際。
草色煙光殘照裏。
無言誰會憑闌意。

擬把疏狂圖一醉。
對酒當歌,
強樂還無味。
衣帶漸寬終不悔。
爲伊消得人憔悴。

Ti the air o *BUTTERFLEES LOU FLOUERS*

Hingin lang on the hie touer in the saft wind,
Ferawa A see the sorra o springtime,
As mirksome kythes the skyline.
Drowie licht abune green gress in the dwynin sun,
Wordless, for whae kens ma feelins, hingin here?

A'd like ti get ram-stam roarin fou,
Raise a gless an sing,
But a gart pleisur's a wersh thing.
My coat an sash are lowse gettin, but A'll ne'er rue it:
The dreein o this dule's warth it for your sake.

To the air of *BUTTERFLIES LOVE FLOWERS*

Leaning long on the high tower in the soft wind,
Faraway I see the sorrow of Spring,
As the skyline turns dark.
Misty light above green grass in the failing sun,
Wordless, for who knows my feelings, leaning here?

I'd like to get recklessly roaring drunk
Raise a glass and sing,
But a forced pleasure's a flavourless thing.
My coat and sash are getting loose, but I'll never regret it:
Suffering this pain is worth it for your sake.

采蓮令

月華收，
雲淡霜天曙。
西征客、
此時情苦。
翠娥執手，
送臨歧、
軋軋開朱戶。
千嬌面、
盈盈佇立，
無言有淚，
斷腸爭忍回顧？

一葉蘭舟，
便恁急槳凌波去。
貪行色、
豈知離緒，
萬般方寸，
但飲恨、
脈脈同誰語？
更回首、
重城不見，
寒江天外，
隱隱兩三煙樹。

Ti the air o *THE POUIN LOTUS SANG*

The mune's licht gaithert in,
Clouds pale in the rimie dawin lift;
For a body traivlin westawa
It's dreich, a time like this;
A beauty bricht, she tuik ma haun,
Convoyed uis ti the road,
An opent the squeckin reid yett:
A bonnie face in a thousan,
Staunin sae gentie, gentie,
Ne'er a word, but greetin,
Hairt-sair, hou cud she thole me lookin back?

A bit leaf o a coble,
Rowit ti sclim the muckle swaws,
Gyte ti be gaun,
Hou wad it ken the dule o twynin,
That filled ilka inch o our hairts a thousan weys?
We drank deep o rue allanerly,
Fair an fond we were, but whae cud we tell?
Then A turnt ma heid,
The toun's touers A saw nae mair:
Cauld watters, enless cairrie,
An twae-thrie trees happit in the haar.

To the air of *THE PULLING LOTUS SONG*

The moon's light was gathered in,
Clouds pale in the frosty dawn skies;
For somebody travelling westward
It's dreary, a time like this;
A beauty bright, she took my hand,
Accompanied me to the road,
And opened the squeaking red gate:
A bonny face in a thousand,
Standing so gentle and dainty,
Never a word, but weeping,
Heart-sore, how could she have endured me looking back?

A tiny leaf of a boat,
Rowed to climb the great waves,
Crazy to be off,
How would it know the pain of parting,
That filled every inch of our hearts a thousand ways?
We drank deep of only regret,
Fair and fond we were, but who could we tell?
Then I turned my head,
The town's towers I saw no more:
Wintry river, endlessly moving clouds,
And two or three trees wrapped in thick fog.

浪淘沙慢

夢覺，
透窗風一線，
寒燈吹息。
那堪酒醒，
又聞空階夜雨頻滴。
嗟因循、
久作天涯客。
負佳人、
幾許盟言，
便忍把、
從前歡會，
陡頓翻成憂戚。

愁極，
再三追思，
洞房深處，
幾度飲散歌闌，
香暖鴛鴦被。
豈暫時疏散，
費伊心力，
殢雲尤雨，
有萬般千種，
相憐相惜。

恰到如今，
天長漏永，
無端自家疏隔。
知何時、
卻擁秦雲態？
願低幃昵枕，
輕輕細說與，
江鄉夜夜，
數寒更思憶。

Ti the air o *SLAW THE WAVES ON THE SAUNS*

Waukenin frae dreams,
A tirl o wind cam throu a crack in ma winnock,
An whifft out the winter cruisie;
Hou can A thole soberin up
Ti hear yince mair the nicht rain
Dreep-dreepin on the cauld steppie-stair?
A sicher the same auld wey,
Owre lang a fremmit bodie at the lift's-en.
A begunkit ma bonnie jo:
Sae monie aiths,
An hou did A dree the brekkin o them,
Turnin aa our blithe an bygane trysts
Ti dule an care in a blink?

When sorra's at its heichest
Owre an owre A mind
Hou aften, deep in the bridal bouer,
     drink taen an singin dune,
We'd coorie in ablow the marra-deuk quilts.
E'en sinderin for a wee while
Brocht her cark an care:
Chaumer-glee o the wantonest,
In hunners, thousans o weys,
For fond an fain wi hairt-likin wir we baith.

But thir days, nou,
Lang's the nichts an weary the unchyngin hourgless –
Whit did A gang an lea her for?
Wha kens when
A'll fin anither pillie-wanton quine;

Aa A want's a bield on the ae bowster inben the bed-hingers,
Ti saftlie tell her,
Hou nicht eftir nicht in watterside clachans,
Throu monie's the cauld hour A thocht lang on her.

To the air of *SLOW THE WAVES ON THE SANDS*

Waking from dreams,
A puff of wind came through a crack in my window,
And blew out the winter lamp;
How can I bear sobering up
To hear once more the night rain
Drip-dripping on the cold stairs?
I sigh the same old way,
Too long a stranger at the ends of the earth.
I jilted my bonny lover:
So many oaths,
And how could I bear the breaking of them,
Turning all our blithe trysts in times gone by
To sorrow and care in the blink of an eye?

When sorrows are at their height
Over and over I recall
How often, deep in the bridal bower,
        drink taken and singing done,
We'd cuddle under the paired-duck quilts.
Even being apart for a little while
Made her anxious and unhappy:
Bedroom fun of the wantonest,
In hundreds, thousands of ways,
For fond and tender with love and affection were we both.

But these days, now,
Long are the nights and weary is the unchanging hourglass –
Why did I go and leave her?
Who knows when
I'll find another pillow-wanton wench;

All I want is shelter on one bolster inside the bed-curtains,
To softly tell her,
How night after night in riverside hamlets,
Through many cold hours I thought long and long on her.

———————————

定風波

自春來、
慘綠愁紅,
芳心是事可可。
日上花梢,
鶯穿柳帶,
猶壓香衾臥。
暖酥消、
膩雲嚲、
終日厭厭倦梳裹。
無那。
恨薄情一去,
音書無個。

早知恁麼,
悔當初、
不把雕鞍鎖。
向雞窗,
只與蠻箋象管,
拘束教吟課。
鎮相隨、
莫拋躲,
針線閒拈伴伊坐。
和我,
免使年少,
光陰虛過。

Ti the air o *SATTLIN WIND AN WAVE*

Sin spring cam,
Wi sair greens an sorrafu reids
Ma hairt hardly keeps a caum souch;
The sun shines on petal-ends,
Yalla-yites gae throu the sauch-shaws,
But A'm still lyin in perfumit quilts;
Ma creishie face cream's meltit in the heat,
The glaizie cloud o ma hair's hingin squint,
Languishin the leelang day, owre weary ti kaim ma hair
    or hap ma heid.
Naethin ti be dune.
A rue him gaun awa, the faithless bodie –
Wittins, or letters – no the yae yin.

A kent lang syne it'd be like this,
An A rue that at the first
A didna lock his fantoosh saiddle awa;
Forenenst the study winnock
Wi fancy paper an ivory pen,
A'd haud back frae scrievin sangs.
Lang an lang A follaed him
A didna forhoo him or jouk him,
In times o idleset A'd tak needle an threid an sit wi him.
Wi me
He didna lichtlie our youthheid,
An thowlessly tine our time.

To the air of *SETTLING WIND AND WAVE*

Since spring came,
With wretched greens and sorrowful reds
My heart's scarcely ever serene;
The sun shines on petal-tips,
Orioles slip through the willow woods,
But I'm still lying in perfumed quilts;
My greasy face cream melted in the heat,
The shiny cloud of my hair hangs askew,
Languishing the livelong day, too weary to comb my hair
    or wrap my head.
Nothing to be done.
I regret him leaving, the faithless one –
News, or letters – not a single thing.

I knew long ago it would be like this,
And I regret that at the beginning
I didn't lock his fancy saddle away;
Before the study window
With fancy paper and ivory pen,
I'd hold back from making songs.
Long, long I followed him
I didn't forsake him or deceive him,
In times of inactivity I'd take needle and thread
    and sit with him.
With me
He didn't take our youth lightly,
Or idly waste our time.

少年游

長安古道馬遲遲，
高柳亂蟬嘶。
夕陽島外，
秋風原上，
目斷四天垂。

歸雲一去無蹤跡，
何處是前期？
狎興生疏，
酒徒蕭索，
不似去年時。

Ti the air o *STRAVAIGIN IN YOUTHHEID*

Slaw's ma pownie on the auld streets o Langpeace Toun,[25]
Hie sauchs gaunin gyte wi wheetlin chairkers,
The settin sun ayont the annay,
Hairst wind on the braes,
An as fer as een can see, a hingy lift in ilka airt.

Clouds win awa an fient the haet o them's left ahint,
Whan'll the twa o's e'er meet again?
Me, A'm out the wey o the huremongerin,
Ma boozy pals are few an faur atween:
It's no like it wis this year bypast.

---

25 Note 21 above.

To the air of *RAMBLING IN YOUTH*

Slow is my pony on the old streets of Longpeace Town,
Tall willows crazy with chirping cicadas,
The setting sun beyond the river island,
Autumn wind on the hillside,
And as far as eye can see, a lowering sky in every direction.

Clouds go away and leave not a trace behind,
When will we two ever meet again?
Me, I'm not used to brothel-visiting,
And boozy pals are few and far between:
It's not like it was this time last year.

———————

戚氏/夢遊仙

晚秋天，
一霎微雨灑庭軒。
檻菊蕭疏，
井梧零亂，
惹殘煙。
淒然，
望江關，
飛雲黯淡夕陽閒。
當時宋玉悲感，
向此臨水與登山。
遠道迢遞，
行人淒楚，
倦聽隴水潺湲。
正蟬吟敗葉，
蛩響衰草，
相應喧喧。

孤館度日如年，
風露漸變，
悄悄至更闌。
長天淨，
絳河清淺，
皓月嬋娟。
思綿綿，
夜永對景，
那堪屈指暗想從前。
未名未祿，
綺陌紅樓，
往往經歲遷延。

帝里風光好，
當年少日，
暮宴朝歡。
況有狂朋怪侶，
遇當歌對酒竟留連。
別來迅景如梭，
舊游似夢，
煙水程何限？
念利名、
憔悴長縈絆，
追往事、
空慘愁顏。
漏箭移，
稍覺輕寒，
漸嗚咽、
畫角數聲殘。
對閑窗畔，
停燈向曉，
抱影無眠。

Ti the air o *MAISTER QI*,
or TRAIVLIN WI TRANSCENDANDS IN DREAMS

Hairst-en,
A smirr o rain splatters the windaes,
No monie chrysanths left bi the palins,
An the guddle o planetree leafs about the well
Is happit in the lest o the haar;
Dowie an wae,
A look ti the Watter an the Mairches,
The fleein cairrie derknin wi the dwnyin sun's retiral;
Song Yu was sair vext yon time
He cam here to sclim the bens an ride the watters,
Hyne awa on his lang road,
Sae wearilie he heard the gurly waters rinnin.[26]
Chairkers wheetle in hotts o faa'n leafs,
An crickets squeck in the failin gress,
Answerin ilkither, gleg as a cried fair.

In the lanesome chynge-hous yae day weirs awa like a year,
Wind an weet are caller gettin,
It's lown an lown in the howe o the nicht;
The lang lift clears,
The White Strip's aa licht
An the bricht mune's braw.
Drawn-out an fanklt's ma hairt's care,
Thru the enless nicht A sit forenent ma shedda,
An canna thole ti count it aa on ma fingers,

---

26 Song Yu (fl. 298-263BCE). Poet, traditionally credited with authorship of some
of the poems in *Songs of the South* (*Chu Ci*), and believed to have been the poet who
first introduced the use of themes and images from the natural world.

But A think in dern on bygane times.
A hed naither rank nor riches,
But on bonnie causeys an in gentie bordels
A sottert about wi the lassies as the years wure awa.

Grand's the scenes o the City Imperial,
An in the days o ma youthheid,
It wis aa soirees an drinkin, frae morn ti nicht;
Mairatowre, wi brilliant billies an byornar freins,
Splorin an singin, an the drams we wir sae sweir ti gie owre.
Time shuttlt by in an eeblink,
An nou the auld gallivants are like a dream:
Hou lang's the road o rouks an watters?
Thinkin on fame an gaithert gear,
Is but a lestin langle ti mak ye shilpit an pale,
An chasin eftir times bypast
Gies ye a doolfu face for naethin.
The watter-knock's haun gangs like an arra,
An A'm feelin the cauld a wee bit mair,
Stertin ti sab an girn
As the soun o the watchie's pentit horn fades awa:
Sittin forenent ma lanesome winnock,
A smoor the lantern, wait on the dawin,
Waukrife, oxterin ma ain shedda.

To the air of *MASTER QI, or TRAVELLING WITH TRANSCENDENTS IN DREAMS*

Late autumn,
Drizzling rain splashes the windows,
Not many chrysanthemums left by the fence,
And the muddle of sycamore leaves around the well
Is shrouded in the last of the fog;
Doleful and full of sorrow,
I look to the Water and the Marches,
The flying clouds darkening with the setting sun's retreat;
Song Yu was sorely vexed the time
He came here to climb the hills and ride the waters,
Far away on his long journey,
So wearily he heard the stormy waters running.
Cicadas chirp in heaps of fallen leaves,
And crickets squeak in the failing grass,
Merry and busy they cry to each other.

In the lonely change-house one day wears away like a year,
Wind and rain are getting fresher,
It's silent at the dead of night;
The long sky clears,
The Milky Way is all light
And the bright moon is lovely.
Drawn-out and tangled is my heart's care,
Through the endless night I sit across from my shadow,
And cannot bear to count it all on my fingers,
But secretly I think of bygone times.
I had neither rank nor riches,
But on handsome streets and in genteel brothels
A messed about with the girls as the years wore away.

Grand were the scenes of the City Imperial,
And in the days of my youth,
It was all parties and drinking, from morning to night;
Moreover, with brilliant pals and extraordinary friends,
Making merry, singing, drinking we were
        so reluctant to give up.
Time shuttled by in the blink of an eye,
And now the old gallivanting is like a dream:
How long is the road of mist and water?
Thinking of fame and gathered goods,
Is just an eternal tether to keep you sickly and pale,
And chasing after times past
Gives you a doleful face for nothing.
The water-clock's hand goes like an arrow,
And I'm feeling the cold a little more,
Starting to whimper and sob
As the sound of the watchman's painted horn fades away:
Sitting before my lonely window,
I put out the lantern, wait for dawn,
Wide awake, hugging my own shadow.

夜半樂

凍雲黯淡天氣，
扁舟一葉，
乘興離江渚。
度萬壑千岩，
越溪深處。
怒濤漸息，
樵風乍起，
更聞商旅相呼。
片帆高舉，
泛畫鷁、
翩翩過南浦。

望中酒旆閃閃，
一簇煙村，
數行霜樹。
殘日下、
漁人鳴榔歸去。
敗荷零落，
衰楊掩映。
岸邊兩兩三三，
浣紗游女，
避行客、
含羞笑相語。

到此因念，
繡閣輕拋，
浪萍難駐。
嘆後約叮嚀竟何據？
慘離懷、
空恨歲晚歸期阻。
凝淚眼、
杳杳神京路，
斷鴻聲遠長天暮。

Ti the air o *BLITHE AT MIDNICHT*

Geelit clouds, an oorie lift,
The wee coble's a bit leaf,
Whan A tak a norie ti lea the annay;
Ten thousan cleuchs an a thousan skerrs gaun by,
As A lea ahint the stream's deepest airts,
Beilin swaws slawlike settle,
On a sudden the Muckle Forester gell sterts ti blaw,
An A hear the packmen hoo-hoo ti ilkither.
The yae sail's heizit up
An awa snooves the hern-stemmit coble,[27]
Licht an licht crossin ti the southron haugh.

A get a ferawa swatch o dramshop pinsels
In reekie clachans,
An a wheen raws o frostit trees.
Ablow a deein sun
Hame-gaun fishers gar their rungs dirl;[28]
Fushionless lotuses gizzen an faa,
Dwynin sauchs play keekie-bo,
In twaesomes an thriesomes alang the braes,
Flindrikin claes new-wuishen, promenadin lasses
Evite the passin stranger,
Bletherin ti ilkither wi blate wee smiles.

Come ti this airt, fine A mind
Hou lichtlie A forhooiet her flourist bouer:
Driftin deuk's-weed's ill ti stap.

---

27 A heron's head was painted on the bows of fishing boats, to bring the heron's luck to the boat.
28 i.e. they knock their sticks together to make frightened fish leap into the net.

Eftir the sicherin, the hechts,
But whit grun nou for aa the tellins A gat?
A'm hairt-sair at the twynin,
An vain it is ti rue the bygane years
        whan doutsome's ma hame-gaun.
Tearfu een steikit, A see
Hou derk an mirksome's the road ti the Halie Citie:
Ferawa a tint swan-guse is craikin in the lang gloamin lift.

To the air of *BLITHE AT MIDNIGHT*

Freezing clouds, a gloomy sky,
The little rowing boat's just a leaf,
When I take a notion to leave the river island;
Ten thousand ravines and a thousand cliffs go by,
As I leave behind the stream's deepest parts,
Angry waves slowly settle,
On a sudden the Great Forester gale starts to blow,
And I hear the packmen call out to each other.
A single sail is hoisted up
And away slips the heron-stemmed boat,
Lightly crossing to the southern bank.

I get a distant glimpse of tavern pennants
In smoky hamlets,
And rows of frosted trees.
Below a dying sun
Homeward bound fishermen bang their sticks together;
Dry lotuses wither and fall
Failing willows play peek-a-boo,
In twos and threes along the banks,
Gauzy clothes new-washed, promenading lasses
Dodge the passing stranger,
Chattering to each other with shy little smiles.

Arrived here, well I remember
How lightly I abandoned her bedecked bower:
Drifting duckweed is impossible to stop.
After the sighs, the promises,
What was the reason for all the scoldings I got?
I'm heartbroken at this parting,

And it's vain to regret the bygone years
    when my homecoming is doubtful.
Tearful eyes shut, I see
How dark and obscure is the road to the Holy City:
Far away a lost swan-goose is calling in the long twilight sky.

———————————

玉蝴蝶

望處雨收雲斷，
憑闌悄悄，
目送秋光。
晚景蕭疏，
堪動宋玉悲涼。
水風輕、
蘋花漸老；
月露冷、
梧葉飄黃。
遣情傷，
故人何在？
煙水茫茫。

難忘。
文期酒會，
幾孤風月，
屢變星霜。
海闊山遙，
未知何處是瀟湘？
念雙燕、
難憑音信；
指暮天、
空識歸航。
黯相望，
斷鴻聲裏，
立盡斜陽。

Ti the air o *JOWELT BUTTERFLEES*

A look an see the rain's devault an the clouds skailt,
A hing quietlike on the raivlin,
Een stellit on the hairst-time scene.
The gloamin looks that dreich an dour,
It wad gar e'en Song Yu greit an mane.[29]
Licht's the wind on the watter,
Deuk's-weed flouers auld gettin,
Dew cauld under the mune's licht,
Planetree leafs waggin yella.
It's sair when hairt-likin chynges,
An whaur about's ma jo?
Enless, enless, the rouk an the watters.

Ill ti forget,
The pairties, the singin an the drammin:
Wanworthie wis A o thae braw days an bonnie scenes,
As yin an bi yin the years wure awa.
Braid's the sea an hyneawa the hills,
A kenna whaur ti fin the airt A lang for.
A dout thae twa swallas
Canna be lippent til for wittins for us:
A pynt at the gloaming lift,
Kennin the road hame's uiseless.
But A look there, disjaskit —
An wi the craikin o a tint swan-guse
A've stude here the haill lang dayset.

---

29 See note 25 above.

To the air of *JEWELLED BUTTERFLIES*

I look and see the rain has stopped and the clouds scattered,
I lean quietly on the railing,
Eyes fixed on the autumn scene.
The dusk looks so desolate and dreary,
It would make even Song Yu weep and wail.
Light is the wind on the water,
Duckweed flowers getting old,
Dew cold under the moonlight,
Sycamore leaves wagging yellow.
It's hard when love changes,
And where is my lover?
Endless, endless, the mist and the water.

Impossible to forget,
The parties, the singing and the drinking:
I wasn't worthy of these beautiful days and lovely scenes,
As one by one the years wore away.
Broad's the sea and far the hills,
I don't know where to find the place I long for.
I doubt that these two swallows
Can't be trusted for news for us:
I point at the twilight sky,
Knowing the way home is useless.
But I look there, disconsolate –
And with the cries of a lost swan-goose
I've stood here the whole long sunset.

八聲甘州/瀟瀟雨

對瀟瀟暮雨灑江天，
一番洗清秋。
漸霜風淒緊，
關河冷落，
殘照當樓。
是處紅衰翠減，
苒苒物華休。
惟有長江水，
無語東流。

不忍登高臨遠，
望故鄉渺邈，
歸思難收。
嘆年來蹤跡，
何事苦淹留？
想佳人、
妝樓顒望，
誤幾回、
天際識歸舟？
爭知我、
倚闌干處，
正恁凝愁。

Ti the air o *GANZHOU SANG ECHT*
or *CALLER, CALLER RAIN*

A face the mirksome gloamin, rain plashin on the watter,
Weshin caller hairst-time clean.
Snell winds are caulder gettin,
Mairchlan hills an burns lown an still,
As the lest o the licht shines inti the laft.
Here's aa failin reids an tint greens,
As houlie an slaw the beauty o aathing devauls.
The swaws o the Lang Watter alane
Rin eastawa, sayin naethin.

A canna thole sclimmin up ti look awa out
Ti see ma auld hyneawa hame,
But thochts o hame-gaun are ill ti pit by.
A sicher at the road A tuik thae years bypast,
But hou am A this sweirt ti win awa?
A think o ma bonnie jo
Lookin fer awa frae the weimenfowk's laft,
Monie times miskennin
Ma hame-comin coble at the lift's en.
Hou wad she ken that me,
A'm hingin on a raivlin tae,
Wi the same hairt-sair sorrae?

To the air of *GANZHOU SONG EIGHT* or *FRESH, FRESH RAIN*

I face the darkening twilight, rain splashing on the river,
Washing fresh autumn clean.
Sharp winds are getting colder,
Borderland hills and streams silent and still,
As the last of the light shines into the loft.
Here it's all failing red and faded green,
As softly and slowly the beauty of everything is lost.
The waves of the Long Water alone
Run eastward, saying nothing.

I can't abide climbing up to look out
To see my old far-away home,
But thoughts of home-coming are hard to put aside.
I sigh at the road I took these last years,
But why am I so unwilling to leave?
Looking far away from the womenfolk's loft,
Many times mistaken about
My home-coming boat at the sky's end.
How would she know that me,
I'm leaning on a railing too,
With the same heart-broken sorrow?

———————————

迷神引

一葉扁舟輕帆卷，
暫泊楚江南岸。
孤城暮角，
引胡笳怨。
水茫茫，
平沙雁。
旋驚散。
煙斂寒林簇，
畫屏展，
天際遙山小，
黛眉淺。

舊賞輕拋，
到此成遊宦。
覺客程勞，
年光晚。
異鄉風物，
忍蕭索，
當愁眼。
帝城賒，
秦樓阻，
旅魂亂。
芳草連空闊，
殘照滿，
佳人無消息，
斷雲遠。

Ti the air o *BEGLAMOURT OWRECOME*

A bit leaf o a coble, licht sail disriggit,
Lyin at anker for a wee on the south bank o the Caller Burn.
Forenicht horns frae the Lane Peel
Gar Tartar shawms girn in repone.
A vast o watter,
Geese on the links,
That glifft, birl an skail.
The haar lifts owre beltins o cauld shaws,
A pentit screen openin up:
Fer hills, smaa at the lift's en,
Faa awa like pentit eebrous.

Lichtlie A cast awa aathing that gleddent uis afore,
An thir days A'm become a banisst officeman;
Traivel's sair, A fin,
As A'm weirin on in years.
The sichts o a fremmit toun
Ti me are dreich an dour,
Like tears in ma sorrafu een.
The Citie Imperial's hyneawa,
A'm sindert frae ma bonnie jo,
An ma wandert sowl's fair raivelt.
Sweet gress raxes the lenth o the braid lands,
Steept in failin licht,
But the're nae wittins o ma lovie,
An ferawa's the skailt clouds.

To the air of *BEWITCHED REFRAIN*

A little leaf of a boat, light sail unrigged,
Lying at temporary anchor on the south bank
    of the Caller Stream.
Evening horns from the Lone Tower
Make Tartar shawms whine in response.
A vast expanse of water,
Geese on the sands,
That whirl and scatter when they're startled.
The thick fog lifts above belts of cold woodland,
A painted screen opening up:
Far hills, small on the skyline,
Fall away like painted eyebrows.

Lightly I threw away everything that gladdened me before,
And these days I've become a banished official;
Travel's hard, I find,
As I'm wearing on in years.
The sights of an unfamiliar town
To me are dull and dreary,
Like tears in my sorrowful eyes.
The City Imperial is far distant,
I'm parted from my bonny lover,
My wandered soul's disordered and confused.
Sweet grass reaches all the broad land,
Steeped in failing light,
But there's no news of my lover,
And far away are the scattered clouds.

竹馬子

登孤壘荒涼，
危亭曠望，
靜臨煙渚。
對雌霓掛雨，
雄風拂檻，
微收煩暑。
漸覺一葉驚秋，
殘蟬噪晚，
素商時序。
覽景想前歡，
指神京、
非霧非煙深處。

向此成追感，
新愁易積，
故人難聚。
憑高盡日凝佇，
贏得消魂無語。
極目霽靄霏微，
暝鴉零亂，
蕭索江城暮。
南樓畫角，
又送殘陽去。

Ti the air o *BAMBOO HORSIE*

Up A sclimmed ti a lane scabbit knowe,
Hyneawa A look frae the bothy at the tap:
It's lythe an lown outowre the roukie annays.
The're rain faain yit forenent the wattergaw,
An a rouch wind shogs the raivlin:
It's the lest o the simmer's heat.
A stert ti feel the leaf's gliff at the hairst,
Chairkers whitter yit at een,
Tho the sun's timeously turnt pale an wan.
The yae scance o the scene minds uis o bygane joys,
An A pynt at the Halie Citie,
But deep in rouk an haar, it's ill ti see.

Forenent this A backart glance:
Ma new cares are easy ingaithert,
Ma auld friens ill ti forgaither wi.
Up A sclimmed the haill day, ti staun still
Whummelt wi sorra, wi nae words ti tell.
As fer as A can see it's aa rouks an drows,
A pickle corbies guddlin about in the gloamin:
The waterside toun's dreich at een,
Frae the Southron Touer the pentit horns blaw,
Ti yince mair convoy the dwynin sun ti rest.

To the air of *BAMBOO HORSIE*

Up I climbed to a lone scabby knoll,
Far I look from the cabin at the peak:
It's quiet and still out over the misty river islands.
There's still rain falling front of the rainbow,
And a rough wind shakes the railing:
It's the last of the summer's heat.
I begin to feel the leaf's surprise at the autumn,
Cicadas still chirp at evening,
Though on time the sun has turned pale and wan.
A single scan of the scene reminds me of bygone joys,
And I point to the Holy City,
But deep in mist and fog, it's hard to see.

Faced with this I backward glance:
My new cares are easily gathered in,
My old friends hard to meet.
Up I climbed the whole day, to stand still
Overwhelmed with sorrow, with no words to tell.
As far as I can see it's all mist and drizzle,
A few crows straggling about in the twilight:
The waterside town's dreary at evening,
From the Southern Tower the painted horns blow,
To convey the setting sun to rest again.

———

臨江仙

夢覺小庭院,
冷風淅淅,
疏雨瀟瀟。
綺窗外,
秋聲敗葉狂飄。
心搖。
奈寒漏永,
孤幃悄,
淚燭空燒。
無端處,
是繡衾鴛枕,
閒過清宵。

蕭條。
牽情繫恨,
爭向年少偏饒。
覺新來、
憔悴舊日風標。
魂消。
念歡娛事,
煙波阻、
後約方遙。
還經歲,
問怎生禁得,
如許無聊

Ti the air o *WATTERSIDE TRANSCENDANDS*

Waukent frae dreams in the wee back court,
Cauld wind reishle-reishlin,
The rap-rap o smaa rain ayont the dyke.
Out the astragal winnock,
The soun o faa'n leafs in the gurly wind's the soun o hairst.
Ma hairt shoogles,
Tholin the cauld an the morn-come-ne'er watter-clock,
In the lythe o the lanesome bed-hingers,
The caunle's tears wir brunt awa for naethin.
Whit for
Did the broidert quilt an marra-deuk bowster
Pass wi me this uiseless nicht?

It's hard.
A think on, an A rue
Hou proud an fantoosh A wis in youthheid.
Nou A newlins find
Ma face cruppen-in an shilpit, bonnie nae mair.
Ma sowl eelies awa,
An A mind on bygane joys,
Gane like haar aff the watter.
Fer awa an aye unsure are biddins yit ti come.
But A'll win throu ti anither year,
Ti speir hou cud A thole
A time sae lang an weary.

To the air of *RIVERSIDE TRANSCENDENTS*

Woken from dreams in the little back courtyard,
Cold wind rustle-rustling,
The rap-rap of small rain beyond the wall.
Outside the traceried window,
The sound of fallen leaves in the gusty wind
      is the sound of autumn.
My heartbeat's unsteady,
Enduring the cold and the morning-come-never water-clock,
In the shelter of the lonely bed-curtains,
The candle's tears were burnt away for nothing.
Why
Did the embroidered quilt and paired drake and duck bolster
Pass with me this useless night?

It's hard.
I think on, and I regret
How proud and fancy I was in youth.
Now for the first time I find
My face shrunk and skinny, bonny no more.
My soul slips away,
And I recall bygone joys,
Gone like mist off the water.
Far away and still unsure are invitations still to come.
But I'll survive to another year,
To ask how I could endure
A time so long and weary.

王安石
WANG ANSHI (1021-1086)

An extremely important politician and economic reformer who rose to Assistant Revenue Commissioner in the State Finance Commission after a successful career in the provinces. He is recognised as one of the great prose writers of the age, and, with Ouyang Xiu, one of the arbiters of literary taste. His poetry is technically skilled, with an emphasis on precise diction, as well as on the social utility of literature: he wrote few *ci*, but many old-style *shi*, and "protest" poems which have led to comparisons with the great 8th century master, Du Fu (712-770).

桂枝香

登臨送目，
正故國晚秋，
天氣初肅。
千里澄江似練，
翠峰如簇。
歸帆去棹殘陽裏，
背西風，
酒旗斜矗。
彩舟雲淡，
星河鷺起，
畫圖難足。

念往昔、
繁華競逐，
嘆門外樓頭，
悲恨相續。
千古憑高，
對此漫嗟榮辱。
六朝舊事隨流水，
但寒煙、
芳草凝綠。
至今商女，
時時猶唱，
《後庭》遺曲。

Ti the air o *A WAFF O CANNEL BEUCHS*

A sclimmed up ti look out as fer as A cud see,
An there wis the umwhile kinrik at hairst-en,
The weather juist snell gettin.
For a thousan mile the clear Watter's like a snood o white,
The emerant taps like a posy o flouers.
Cobles rowin hame in the gaun-doun sun,
Their backs to the wast wind;
Dram-pensils waffin heich an squint,
Buskit boats pale forenenst the cairrie,
The White Strip risin abune Hern Annay:
A pentit picture cudna dae it justice.

A mind langsyne,
Whan gentrice wad kemp an tulyie,
An A sich an sab that on touer-heids an outbye the ports
Sicna sorras are even-on dreeit yit.
Gin fowk sclimmed up hie a thousan year syne
Whit shame or glory wad they hae seen here?
Aa the trokin o the Sax Kinriks, gane like rinnin watter,[30]
The're juist cauld haar an dwynin gress o derk green.
Nou aye an on the sangster-lassies chant
Haunit-doun ballants frae the Royal Weimens' Haas.

---

30 The Six Dynasties (220-589 or 222-589) a chaotic period of disunion and civil war.

To the air of *A WHIFF OF CINNAMON BOUGHS*

I climbed up to look out as far as I could see,
And there was the former kingdom at autumn's end,
The weather just getting sharp.
For a thousand miles the clear River's like a ribbon of white,
The emerald peaks like a posy of flowers.
Small boats row home in the setting sun,
Their backs to the west wind;
Tavern pennants flapping high and slanting,
Decorated boats pale before the moving clouds,
The Milky Way rising above Heron Island:
A painted picture couldn't do it justice.

I remember long ago,
When the gentry would contend and brawl,
And I sigh and sob that on tower-tops and before city gates
Such sorrows are continually suffered still.
If people climbed up high a thousand years ago
What shame or glory would they have seen here?
All the nefarious dealings of the Six Dynasties,
      gone like running water,
There's only cold mist and withering grass of dark green.
Now the singing-girls continuously chant
Handed-down ballads from the Royal Women's Halls.

———————

千秋歲引

別館寒砧，
孤城畫角，
一派秋聲入寥廓。
東歸燕從海上去，
南來雁向沙頭落。
楚臺風，
庾樓月，
宛如昨。

無奈被些名利縛，
無奈被他情擔擱，
可惜風流總閒卻。
當初漫留華表語，
而今誤我秦樓約。
夢闌時，
酒醒後，
思量著。

Ti the air o
THE OWRECOME O A THOUSAN HAIRSTS

Cauld waulk-stanes as we pairt at the chynge-hous,
Pentit horns on the Lane Peel,
A clamjamfry o hairst-time souns in the tuim outbye.
Eastawa hame-gaun swallas come frae the sea,
Southawa-boun wild geese drap doun ti the sauns,
The wind on the Southron Deas,[31]
The mune owre the Laird o Girnel's Laft,[32]
A mind them like yestreen.

A cudna help thirlin masel ti siller an name,
A cudna help taiglin wi an auld luve,
It's a peety ma gallivantin days are owre aathegither.
Back then A dawdled lang afore the scrievins
    on the Pentit Stoups,[33]
Nae hecht ti me in a Jowel Laft wis e'er hadden til:[34]
When dreams hae dwynit,
An when A'm waukent frae drink,
A'll be thinkin lang.

---

31 Allusion to where a King of Chu once met and made love to a divine woman, so generally a place of assignations, where men and women could meet and mingle.
32 A building in Jiujiang, Jiangsu Province, once believed to have been built by general Yu Liang (289-340CE).
33 Ornamental columns erected in front of palaces, temples, etc., usually decorated with parallel couplets.
34 That is, an elegant apartment, a singing-girl's rooms, or a brothel.

To the air of
THE REFRAIN OF A THOUSAND AUTUMNS

Cold fulling blocks as we part at the change-house,
Painted horns on the Lone Tower,
A commotion of autumn sounds in the empty outskirts.
Eastwards home-going swallows come from the sea,
Southward-bound wild geese drop down to the sands,
The wind on the Dais of Chu,
The moon over the Lord Yu's Loft,
I recall them like it was last night.

I couldn't help binding myself to money and fame,
I couldn't help lingering with an old love,
It's a pity my gallivanting days are altogether over.
Back then I dawdled long in front of the writing
        on the Painted Pillars,
No promise to me in a Jewelled Loft was ever kept:
When dreams have faded,
And when I'm sober,
I'll be thinking long.

王安國
WANG ANGUO (1030-1076)

Wang Anshi's younger brother.[35] He held posts in the School for the Sons of the State, and in the Imperial Historiography Institute, whose task was to compile, edit, and revise the official dynastic histories. Two collections of his *ci* survive.

---

35 In the polygamous society of Imperial China, keeping track of family relationships could be complicated, so the habit grew of giving all the male members of one generation a shared syllable of their personal name, which helped to differentiate cousins from uncles, for instance. Wang Anguo's dates are given by some authorities as 1028-74.

清平樂

留春不住，
費盡鶯兒語。
滿地殘紅宮錦污，
昨夜南園風雨。

小憐初上琵琶，
曉來思繞天涯。
不肯畫堂朱戶，
春風自在楊花。

Ti the air o *LOWN PLEISURS*

Nae wey ti kep the spring, for it winna bide.
It's fair wastrife o the lintie's sang.[36]
Dowit reid's slaistert aa owre like palace brocade,
Eftir yestreen's wind an rain in the Southren Gairden.

Wee Lovie the sangster lassie's juist stertit at the lute;[37]
When the dawin comes, A think lang on him at the warld's en.
No willin ti come ti pentit haas an yetts o crammasy,
The spring wind's contentit wi the sauch palmies.

---

36 Naturalised oriole.
37 The 琵琶 *pipa* is indeed a 4-string lute which possibly originated in Central
Asia: as it went west to Persia, the Middle East, and eventually Europe, it gained
more strings and a rounder belly; in the east it kept its slimmer pear-shaped body.

To the air of *TRANQUIL PLEASURES*

No way to keep the spring, for it won't stay.
It's a complete waste of the oriole's song.
Faded red is splattered all around like palace brocade,
After last night's wind and rain in the South Garden.

Little Lovie the singing girl has just started on the lute;
When the dawn comes, I think long on him at the ends of the earth.
Unwilling to come to painted halls and gates of crimson,
The spring wind is content with willow catkins.

———————

晏幾道
YAN JIDAO (1031-1106)

The last distinguished virtuoso of the Southern Tang style, he was praised for his originality (eccentricity, even), and for the nostalgic tone of his refined aristocratic style. 258 of his *ci* survive. Details of his life are scanty, but he appears to have been an aristocrat who squandered his inheritance, drifted from one minor civil service post to another, and died in genteel poverty.

臨江仙

夢後樓臺高鎖，
酒醒簾幕低垂。
去年春恨卻來時，
落花人獨立，
微雨燕雙飛。

記得小蘋初見，
兩重心字羅衣。
琵琶弦上說相思，
當時明月在，
曾照彩雲歸。

Ti the air o *WATTERSIDE TRANSCENDANDS*

Steikit in the hie laft an waukent frae dreamin,
A sober up frae the drink,
     an pull the bed-curtains laich doun.
Yon spring fasherie o years bygane is back,
A bodie staunin her lane mang faain flouers,
As swallas flee in twaesomes throu the smaa rain.

A mind when first A forgaithert wi Wee Soukie,[38]
She wure a flindrikin goun wi doublt pirlicue collars;
On the lute's thairms she spak o hairt-likin,
An bricht wis the munelicht then,
Like it shone frae the clouds when she gaed.

---

38 A singing-girl's soubriquet.

To the air of *RIVERSIDE TRANSCENDENTS*

Shut in the high loft and wakened from dreams,
I sober up from the drink, and pull the bed-curtains
     low down.
That spring trouble from years ago is back,
Somebody standing alone among falling flowers,
As swallows fly in pairs through the fine drizzle.

I remember when first I got together with Little Clover,
She wore a flimsy gown with twin-curlicue collars;
On the lute strings she spoke of true love,
And bright was the moonlight then,
Like it shone from the clouds when she went.

蝶戀花

夢入江南煙水路，
行盡江南，
不與離人遇。
睡裏消魂無說處，
覺來惆悵消魂誤。

欲盡此情書尺素，
浮雁沉魚，
終了無憑據。
卻倚緩弦歌別緒，
斷腸移破秦箏柱。

Ti the air o *BUTTERFLEES LOU FLOUERS*

A dreamed A wis on the roukie watters o the Southlans:[39]
A traivlt the haill o the Southlans,
But ne'er did A forgaither wi her that's gane.
Ma sowl eeliet awa in sleep, words canna tell o't,
An A waukent dowie an wae, begunkit bi ma eeliet-awa sowl.

A wantit shot o thon feelin wi scrievin a letter on white silk,
But neither fleein geese nor doukin fish
Can A lippen til ti tak it, in the hinner en.
A stap the slaw thairms an sing the pain o pairtin,
Stouns in ma wame like zither-trees snappin.

---

39 "South of the River": still the appellation for the lands south of the Yangtze River
and its delta.

To the air of *BUTTERFLIES LOVE FLOWERS*

I dreamed I was on the misty waters of the Southlands:
I travelled all over the Southlands,
But I never did encounter her that's gone.
My soul vanished away in sleep, words can't tell it,
And I woke doleful and grieving, cheated by my
      vanished soul.

I wanted rid of that feeling by writing a letter on white silk,
But neither flying geese nor diving fish
Can I trust to take it, in the final end.
I stop the slow strings and sing the pain of parting,
Pains in my belly like zither bridges snapping.

蝶戀花

醉別西樓醒不記，
春夢秋雲，
聚散真容易。
斜月半窗還少睡，
畫屏閑展吳山翠。

衣上酒痕詩裏字，
點點行行，
總是淒涼意。
紅燭自憐無好計，
夜寒空替人垂淚。

Ti the air o *BUTTERFLEES LOU FLOUERS*

Fou, A bade fareweill at the Wast Laft,
    an cudna mind it whan A woke,
For it wis gane like spring dreams or hairst-time clouds:[40]
In trowth, meetin an twinin's owre easy.
It's ill sleepin wi a sklentin mune fillin hauf the winnock,
The pentit screens are lowsed, the Etin Hills are green.

Tashes o wine on ma goun, the words o a poem,
Ilka tash an ilka line,
They'll aye bear a sense dreich an dour.
The reid caunle peeties itsel, but naethin can it dae,
In the cauld nicht ma vain tears faa for somebody.

---

40 These terms have erotic associations.

To the air of *BUTTERFLIES LOVE FLOWERS*

Tipsy, I said goodbye at the West Loft,
    and couldn't remember when I woke,
For it was gone like spring dreams or autumn clouds:
In truth, meeting and parting are too easy.
It's impossible to sleep with a slanting moon
    filling half the window,
The painted screens are opened, the Giant Hills are green.

Stains of wine on my gown, the words of a poem,
Every stain and every line,
They'll always bear a dull and dreary sense.
The red candle pities itself, but nothing can it do,
In the cold night my vain tears fall for somebody.

———————————

鷓鴣天

彩袖殷勤捧玉鍾,
當年拚卻醉顏紅。
舞低楊柳樓心月,
歌盡桃花扇底風。

從別後,
憶相逢,
幾回魂夢與君同。
今宵剩把銀缸照,
猶恐相逢是夢中。

Ti the air o *PAIRTRICK WEATHER*

Skyrie-Sleeve, ye eidently passed the jowelt quaich,[41]
Willin in thae days, yir tosie cheek wis reid.
In the hairt o sauch an willie lafts for months ye danced,
The sang dune, peach flourish blew awa in the wind.

Eftir we pairtit,
A mindit hou we met,
An monie's the time, sir, ma dreamin sowl wis wi ye.
This nicht the cruisie's kinnelt owre an owre:
Yince mair A'm feart our meetin wis juist a dream.

---

41 A singing-girl's soubriquet.

To the air of *PARTRIDGE WEATHER*

Bright-Sleeve, you diligently passed the jewelled goblet,
Willing in those days, your tipsy cheek was red.
In the heart of poplar and willow lofts
    for months you danced,
The song done, peach blossom blew away in the wind.

After we parted,
I remembered how we met,
And many's the time, sir, my dreaming soul was with you.
Tonight the lamp is lit again and again:
Once more I'm afraid our meeting was just a dream.

————————

鷓鴣天

醉拍春衫惜舊香。
天將離恨惱疏狂。
年年陌上生秋草，
日日樓中到夕陽。

雲渺渺，
水茫茫。
徵人歸路許多長。
相思本是無憑語，
莫向花箋費淚行。

Ti the air o *PAIRTRICK WEATHER*

Fou, A clap yir spring semmits,
     an rue the perfume o times bygane:
Heiven guides meetin an twynin,
     an wis roused at me rinnin ram-stam wud.
Year in, year out, hairst-time gress grows on the bauks,
Day in, day out, in ma laft A bide the dayset.

Dulesome clouds hyneawa,
Wide an wide the watters.
Lang's the road for the hame-gaun traivler.
In the hinner-en the're nae words ti tell o hairt-hunger,
Sae dinna waste yir streikit tears on fantoosh paper.

To the air of *PARTRIDGE WEATHER*

Tipsy, I stroke your spring tunics,
    and rue the perfume of times past:
Heaven guides meetings and partings,
    and was angry at me running wild.
Year in, year out, autumn grass grows on the footpath,
Day in, day out, in my tower I wait for sunset.

Doleful clouds far off,
Wide and wide the waters.
Long's the road for the homecoming traveller.
In the end there are no words to tell of longing,
So don't waste your streaked tears on fancy writing paper.

———————————

生查子

金鞍美少年，
去躍青驄馬。
牽繫玉樓人，
繡被春寒夜。

消息未歸來，
寒食梨花謝。
無處說相思，
背面鞦韆下。

Ti the air o *CALLER HAWS*

A bonnie younker wi a saiddle o gowd,
Skelpin by on a fine lyart pownie.
Whit's he ti dae wi her in her jowel laft,[42]
That's in ablow broidert quilts in the cauld spring nichts?

Nae news e'er cam back ti her,
A pear tree withert bi Cauld Mait Day.[43]
Nae wey ti tell hou she dwynt for luve,
As doun fell the shuggie-shoo ahint her.

---

42 See note 32 above.
43 See note 20 above.

To the air of *FRESH HAWS*

A handsome young man with a saddle of gold,
Cantering by on a fine dappled horse.
What has he to do with her in her jewelled loft,
Who lies under embroidered quilts in the cold spring nights?

No news ever came back to her,
A pear tree withered by Cold Food Day.
No way to tell how she pined away for love,
As down fell the swing behind her.

生查子

關山魂夢長，
塞雁音書少。
兩鬢可憐青，
只為相思老。

歸傍碧紗窗，
說與人人道：
真箇別離難，
不似相逢好。

Ti the air o *CALLER HAWS*

The border hills, a lang road for the dreamin sowl,
A mairchlan guse's letters, few an fer atween;
Pity her wi haffets yince bleck,
Grown auld wi nocht but hairt-hunger.

Back she'll gang ti the emerant silk winnock,
Ti say ti him that wis her jo,
"In verra trowth, pairtin's sair,
An naethin like the joys o meetin".

To the air of *FRESH HAWS*

The border hills, a long road for the dreaming soul,
A frontier goose's letters, few and far between;
Pity her with temples once black,
Grown old with nothing but the heart's yearning.

Back she'll go to the emerald silk window,
To say to him that was her lover,
"In very truth, parting's hard,
And nothing like the joys of meeting".

———————

OWRESETTER'S EIK

I began this book under COVID lockdown, at a loose end, having finished one book[44] of Scots translations while I was waiting for Yang Lian to finish writing the final poems for our next collection *(A Tower Built Downwards)*[45]. I wandered into my living room after breakfast one morning, wondering what I might do next: my eye was caught by *300 Song Ci,*[46] a book I bought in the summer of 1989, when I was working as a translator at Amnesty International's International Secretariat in London. I won't say I had never opened it, but I had never read these beautiful and widely-admired poems *in extenso*, so, on 6th January 2021, I sat down at my desk and began to read.

Although I had translated a few poems of this type for various journals, I had no plan or any preconceived idea of which poets I wanted to translate: I just opened the book at page 1, and started there. Since what we have here is poems

---

44 *Hairst Winds An Hard Roads: Li Bai an Du Fu in Scots* (2022) Edinburgh: Taproot Press.
45 Forthcoming, Bloodaxe Books, Spring 2023.
46 *300 Song Ci* 《宋詞三百首》 ed. Zhu Zumou 朱祖謀 (1924), in the Sanmin Shuju 三民書局 1989 edition, edited and annotated by Wang Zhong 汪中. This is a well-known and widely-used high school textbook. *Ci* is pronounced *tsuh*, and can be translated as "words" or "lyrics".

1-60, I can't and don't claim that this is a comprehensive survey of the genre.

I do hope to follow this volume with others: I toyed with the idea of doing a set of three volumes of 100 poems each, but wasn't at all confident I could find a publisher willing to take that on.

Zhu Zumou (1857-1931), the compiler of *300 Song Ci*, was an old-school mandarin, trained under the Empire, who held various government posts, including a stint at the Hanlin Academy, the Imperial body founded in the 8th century which performed various literary tasks for the court, including drafting edicts, establishing texts and providing orthodox interpretations of the Confucian classics for the Civil Service examinations that selected the administrative, military, and judiciary cadre who ran Imperial China. When the Empire fell and was succeeded by the Republic in 1911, Zhu retired from public service, and lived in seclusion in Shanghai for the rest of his life.

300 Song Ci is patterned after Sun Zhu's standard 18th century anthology *300 Tang Shi*, which in turn emulated the canonical *Shi Jing*, or *Classic of Poetry*[47], which contains 305 poems and was believed to have been edited by Confucius himself. The numbers are approximate: *300 Tang Shi* has more than 300 poems, and there are 310 in *300 Song Ci*.[48]

The poetic genre known as *ci* is also called *changduanju*, "long [and] short lines", which aptly describes its difference from the previously dominant *shi*, or "regulated verse" which has lines of a regular fixed length of either 5 or 7 syllables. *Ci*,

---

47 aka *Book of Songs, Book of Odes,* etc.
48 Chinese numbers of this sort are often approximate: Old China Hands will recognise the Chabuduo Principle here — *chabuduo* often translates as "near enough".

however, shows a pattern of irregular line-lengths, but in fixed patterns: this is not *vers libre*. There are upwards of 800 fixed patterns, each with their own blend of long and short lines, and their unalterable metrical structures. It should be noted here that Classical Chinese versification depends not on vowel length or on stress, but on the fixed pitch contour which every syllable possesses.[49] These are grouped into *Oblique* (/) and *Level* (–) tones, so a typical *cipai* or tune pattern would look like this:

$$/-//--.$$
$$/--,$$
$$/--.$$
$$//--,$$
$$///--.$$
$$//---//,$$
$$-//,$$
$$/--.$$

Rhyme is demanded, either on each line or each couplet, and the second stanza may be, to a greater or lesser extent, a mirror-image of the first. The pattern is fixed, so much so that the verb used is not *xie*, to write, but *tian*, to fill in. The pattern may be repeated. The name of the tune pattern, of course, has no connection with the thematic content of the lyric, and though some *ci* were additionally given titles by their authors, this was not seen as necessary. Nowadays, individual *ci* are identified by

---

49 Modern Standard Chinese ("Mandarin" in its spoken form) has four tones: high level, rising, dipping, and falling, and unstressed toneless vowels too. While we know what was written about tonal prosody, we have no very clear idea what the pitch contours of early mediaeval Chinese syllables were like. The Chinese writing system doesn't mark tones.

the name of the tune pattern and the opening line (and can be so Googled, of course).

The ancestors of the *ci* can be found in ancient Chinese *yuefu* poetry, but its mature presence dates from the 9th century, toward the end of the Tang Dynasty (618-907), and its pre-eminence came in the Song Dynasty which followed (960-1279). *Ci* continued to be written through succeeding dynasties, and still are: Chairman Mao Zedong is regarded as one of the most competent *ci* writers of the 20th century, and his poems are widely quoted today, and Yang Lian has written a metrically flawless *ci* which contains no meaningful semantic content at all.[50]

The tune titles are names of songs, whose tonal pattern and rhyme scheme each *ci* must follow, though the tunes are mostly lost. Surviving tunes point to a four-beat rhythm, which isn't easily discernible at first, but if you listen to the way a blues singer varies the rhythms of his lyrics across a steady four-to-the-bar guitar beat, it might come to close to how these songs may have sounded. Some, at least, of the songs were from Silk Road countries, though the traffic went both ways. From the 8th century and into the 12th, Central Asia was all the rage in fashion, music, dancing, and drinking (imported grape wine was replacing traditional rice beer), while in brothels and teahouses, Central Asian girls were fashionable and expensive.

So, to "fill in" a tune pattern, you choose words with the correct Level or Oblique tone to match the pattern. This is very like what Matthew Fitt did when he wrote *Stairway Til Heiven*, matching his Scots rhythms and rhyme-scheme to the Led Zeppelin song *Stairway To Heaven*:

---

50 *Sway, Concentric Circles* (Bloodaxe Books, 2005), p.78

sei aa the miners that dird
at the hert o the yird
thai work the haill nicht throu tae seven
syne ther's a hole i the lift
at the end o the shift
an thai'r wurkin a back-shift tae heaven[51]

The gendered voice is only one of the difficulties these texts present to the translator: because classical Chinese poetry routinely omits pronouns, both for subjects and for objects, it can often be a matter of guesswork to figure out who is speaking, or who is doing what to whom. Generally, the men tend to be the travellers, and women the ones left waiting at home for the return of their dear one. But it's often unclear, and almost every pronoun in this book is tentative. There may also be dialogue, with a statement by one partner answered in the next stanza by the other. Tense, voice, mood, definiteness, indefiniteness, and number aren't grammatically marked either, so the translator has to supply these. In addition, Chinese has nothing like our capitalisation, so identifying proper names is often problematic – e.g. is it *Palace Close*, or *the /a palace close*? As I have done elsewhere, I have translated place names, trying to stay as close to the etymology of the Chinese name as I can. I do this to offer some kind of connotation to the reader, instead of the blank space of an unfamiliar transliterated toponym. Readers of Chinese will of course recognise allusions and place names in the original text, but they don't need my translations.

I haven't attempted to match the strict rhyme-schemes of the originals, though I have tried to roughly match the line

---

51 See Hubbard, T. ed. (1991) *The New Makars* Edinburgh: Mercat Press, p.180

structure by counting stresses, not always strictly, and I have used other sonic devices, chimes, echoes, half-rhymes, slant rhymes, and siclike things. For example, look at this little Yan Shu lyric:

> A new sang an a bicker o wine,
> Fernyear's weather again an the Stank Deas like afore,
> The sun dwynes westawa at dayset, an when'll it retour?
>
> Flouers faa, an deil the thing ti be dune:
> Yince, A kent the swallas wad win hame again,
> Back an forrit A gaun on ma wee gairden
>   path atween the flouers.

Notice the chiming of *wine, dwyne, again, dune,* and *gairden,* or *afore, retour,* and *flouers.* The Chinese end rhymes are on lines 1-3, and 5-6, all on the same sound, but Chinese, being poor in speech sounds, rhymes with much greater ease than Scots does. I try to compensate with alliteration – see *wine, weather, westawa, wad win hame, wee; Deas, dwynes, dayset, deil, dune; fernyear, flouers, faa, forrit*: these are the sonic structures that bind a poem together to make it something more than a collection of random lines. I hope it partly makes up for the loss of the lilting music of the Chinese, too.

The lyrics presented here are mostly in the *wanyue* or "delicate restraint" style,[52] but they can be heart-wrenchingly sad, with themes of yearning and longing, separation and unrequited love – like Country & Western songs, they are for grown-ups, songs which deal honestly with adult themes of love and loss.

---

52 The *haofang* or "heroic abandon" style was a slightly later development.

This was relatively new for China, where poems of friendship between men had previously been more common. Nor was it new for male poets to speak in the voices of women, though it had never been so widespread or popular before.

These *ci* would have been written to be sung by singing-girls, in the capital, Kaifeng, and in the elegant and urbane cities of the Yangtze Delta, such as Hangzhou, Suzhou, or Yangzhou. Successful singing-girls were the high-class courtesans of the age, skilled professional performers, some recognised as poets in their own right, and were often highly accomplished musicians. In the polygamous society of Imperial China, a singing-girl might be taken up for a while by a rich man of the literati or merchant class, to be supported in her own "jewel loft", or even taken permanently into a household as a concubine or secondary wife. In addition, as mandarins were not allowed to serve in their home province, and were rotated every three years, every city had a large number of well-educated and effectively single men, parted from their loved ones, who would no doubt have found these songs of love and longing very much to their taste.

If you're not familiar with Scots, I suggest you visit *Dictionars o the Scots Leid* at www.dsl.ac.uk, where you will find a history of the language, as well as those two masterworks of scholarship, *The Dictionary of the Older Scots Tongue* and the *Scottish National Dictionary*: the first runs up to 1700, and the second carries the story on to the present day. Each is the size of the OED, and they are free to use. Since they are so readily available, I have not provided a glossary.

In brief, Scots is a west Germanic language, like English, but while Modern Standard English derives from the Midland dialect of Old English spoken in Oxford, Cambridge, and London, Scots descends from the dialect spoken from the Wash northward. As Northumbrian, it came into what is now SE Scotland in the 6th century. Until the accession of King David I in 1124, Gaelic was the prestige language of the Scottish court and the nobility, while Latin was the language of church and law. But over the next few centuries Scots gradually spread to the burghs and the landward areas of South, Central, and East Scotland until, by 1424, it had become the language of the Thrie Estaitis, Scotland's parliament, and thus the language of administration and the law. During the Reformation, conservative Catholic propagandists wrote in Scots, while progressive Reformers chose English, as by the time of the Reformation Parliament in 1560, England's church was a reformed one. A lack of printers in Edinburgh led to the importing of Tyndale's Bible in English, which meant that English slowly became the language of high-register discourse, though Scots never died. We continued – and still continue – to speak, sing, and write poetry in Scots. Although prose has been slower to re-establish itself, social media have made possible a boom in "CyberScots" in half a dozen dialects, from the Northern Isles to Ulster, as these informal communication media open up new areas for creative and novel uses of this ancient and malleable tongue.

In this book I have aimed to present Modern Literary Scots in a Lothian standard with traces of Border variations, as was the practice of the great Makars of the 15th and 16th century. There is no standard spelling for Scots, but I adhere more or less to lightly modified Scots Style Sheet spellings.[53]

---

53 Proposed in Edinburgh in 1947, still controversial, and widely ignored, especially in Glasgow and Dundee. See, for instance, https://electricscotland.com/poetry/purves/Grammer_Style.pdf

My source text, *300 Song Ci*, provides a Modern Stand-
ard Chinese paraphrase, glosses, and notes for each of the po-
ems, which is rationale enough, if it's needed, for the inclusion
in this volume of versions and apparatus in English. Non-Chi-
nese readers will not be aware, however, of the meticulous
and voluminous commentaries with which Classical Chinese
texts were always glossed. This began with the ancient Con-
fucian Classics, and was extended to cover Buddhist sutras,
and later to works of philosophy and literature. My own in-
spiration came also from one of the most original literary
minds Imperial China ever produced, the critic Jin Shengtan
(c.1608-1661). He produced brilliant and highly unorthodox
commentaries on what he called the *Six Works of Genius*, a clear
and impudent allusion to the *Six Classics* of orthodox Confu-
cianism, which candidates for the civil service examinations
had to memorise: he chose the mediaeval vernacular novel *The
Water Margin*,[54] the verse drama, *The Western Chamber*, the 8th
century poetry of Du Fu, Sima Qian's ground-breaking 2nd
century BCE *Historical Records*, the 2,000-year-old *Encounter-
ing Sorrow* by Qu Yuan, and the great 4th century BCE work of
Daoist philosophy *Zhuangzi*, and, remarkably, almost blasphe-
mously, he chose them for their literary qualities alone, and
not the morally uplifting qualities for which the Confucian
pedants of his age permitted them (those that they didn't have
banned, that is). In the case of the first two, he provided those
vernacular masterpieces with annotations and commentaries
in often extremely high-register and abstruse literary language.
His *Water Margin* and *Western Chamber*, with their near-bi-
lingual, almost 3-D structure (like watching a film with the

---

54 Several chapters of which I translated many years ago as *Men o the Mossflow* for
the literary magazines *Cencrastus* and *Edinburgh Review*.

Director's Commentary), were my inspiration for this book, as they were when I was making my two previous collections in Scots, *Staunin Ma Lane* and *Hard Roads and Cauld Hairst Winds*.[55]

What have I learned from my encounter with this poetry? I am lost in admiration for the poets who produced such elegant poems in such a tight and demanding form. A well-executed *ci* has the purity and unforced elegance of Song Dynasty porcelain – an object lesson in how invisible the highest art can be.

My sentimental education is also, to my elderly and slightly creaky surprise, still on-going: I have felt the speaker's pain as I sighed over the haunting beauty of the original Chinese, and I have felt my old heart expand in new directions and unexpected ways. I hope some of that has reached you through my struggle to say things never yet said in Scots.

Love, loss, parting, heartbreak, and yearning are universal, for we are one species, after all, no matter how far apart we may be in time and space. And no matter how different our languages and cultures may seem to be, our hearts all resonate to the same tender, loving frequencies.

If your heart is breaking, dear reader, or your heart was once broken and you still bear the scars of it, I hope you found balm for your hurts here. If you're wholly healthy, happy, and very much in love, I hope you found elegance, beauty, and charm to share with your beloved and add to your stock of blissful moments and memories.

---

55 Incidentally, in a thoughtful and thought-provoking review of *Hard Roads and Cauld Hairst Winds* Johnny Rodger raised the issue of why a book in Scots requires annotations and commentaries in English. I hope I have gone some way to answering that question here, though all too briefly. I hope to take this topic up in more detail at a later date. See https://bellacaledonia.org.uk/2022/03/15/extinction-revival-is-scots-haunted/

The rest of us, well, we'll juist hae ti thole it ti it's better, as my granny Chrissie Young used to say.

Brian Holton
Melrose
June 2021, revised February-April 2022